# life
## swap

# life
# swap

## KRISH KANDIAH

MONARCH
BOOKS

Oxford, UK
& Grand Rapids, Michigan, USA

First published in the UK in 2008 by Monarch Books
(a publishing imprint of Lion Hudson plc),
Wilkinson House, Jordan Hill Road, Oxford OX2 8DR.
Tel: +44 (0)1865 302750 Fax: +44 (0)1865 302757
Email: monarch@lionhudson.com
www.lionhudson.com

ISBN: 978-1-85424-867-1 (UK)
ISBN: 978-0-8254-6198-9 (USA)

Distributed by:
UK: Marston Book Services Ltd, PO Box 269, Abingdon, Oxon OX14 4YN;
USA: Kregel Publications, PO Box 2607, Grand Rapids, Michigan 49501

British Library Cataloguing Data

A catalogue record for this book is available from the British Library.

Printed and bound in Malta by Gutenberg Press.

# contents

A few years ago it dawned on me that everybody past a certain age – regardless of how they look on the outside – pretty much constantly dreams of being able to escape from their lives. They don't want to be who they are any more. They want out. This list includes Thurston Howell the Third, Ann-Margaret, the cast members of *Rent*, Vaclav Havel, space shuttle astronauts and Snuffleupagus. It's universal.

Do you want out? Do you often wish you could be somebody, anybody, other than who you are – the you who holds a job and feeds a family – the you who keeps a relatively okay place to live and who still tries to keep your friendships alive? In other words, the you who's going to remain pretty much the same until the casket?

Douglas Coupland, *Gum Thief*, Bloomsbury, 2007

end

At the end of some films, when the credits begin to roll it is a huge relief. Some movies are so tedious they feel like a custodial sentence, and at the end I fight my way to the exit with the other bored viewers. Sometimes I feel I should be paid to endure to the end, instead of handing over my hard-earned cash at the ticket office.

Other films end on a cliffhanger, and I stay in my seat well past the last credit, desperately hoping for more. I leave slowly, knowing that I could be hanging around for a couple of years for the sequel. But the best films end with everything coming together, and I get that satisfied feeling, as when the last piece of a jigsaw is slotted into position.

Occasionally, in the disappointing movies, I wonder what else is showing and whether anyone would notice if I left Theatre 2 for a toilet break and returned to a seat in Theatre 4. Swapping films may not be considered entirely honourable, but it might be a better use of my time and money.

What happens if the disappointing movie is your life? You know there are other films on and you have a sneaking suspicion that they might be better than the one you are currently stuck in. They might at least be worth a quick look.

*Lifeswap* offers a quick look at another kind of life. It is a fly-on-the-wall docudrama on – arguably – the most significant person who has ever lived. It tracks Jesus through the words of one of his eyewitness biographers and watches as he offers lifeswaps to people stuck in all sorts of life movies. Some are tragedies; some are comedies; some are love stories; some are thrillers, but they all have a twist in the tale: a lifeswap that helps these lives to end well.

I want to give you a sneak preview of the end of this docudrama, so you know exactly where we are heading. Some of the biographer's last words are:

> **// Jesus did many other miraculous signs in the presence of his disciples, which are not recorded in this book. But these are written that you may believe that Jesus is the Christ, the Son of God, and that by believing you may have life in his name. //**
> **(John 20:30–31)**

Far from being a spoiler, this describes the biography as a springboard into life. Of course, being alive is normally the minimum requirement for reading a book in the first place, so this must be another life that is available to us – a life offered by Jesus that can make it seem as though we weren't truly alive before. An offer that sounds this good should definitely be explored in more detail. So let's dive in...

# dive

## Can I hope for more?

## Wesley

A crowded metro platform. New York City. Nineteen-year-old Cameron awaits his train. Suddenly a convulsion causes him to lose his balance and he falls onto the tracks. The driver of the oncoming train sees the young man fall and immediately slams on his brakes. But it is too little too late. The train is travelling too fast and is simply unstoppable in the time and distance available. Wesley Autrey, waiting at the same New York metro station with his daughters, knows there isn't a second to lose. Without hesitation, the fifty-year-old construction worker dives off the platform. He pushes Cameron into the gap between the tracks and flings his own body on top of him. Meanwhile, the onlookers watch in horror as the careering train thunders into the station, brakes screeching. As it finally grinds to a halt, there is a moment of silence as helpers cautiously look to see what has happened to the two men. The train had passed inches over their heads: Wesley had saved Cameron's life.

This is not an action set piece from a Hollywood blockbuster. This is a true story. It so impressed New Yorkers that many, including billionaire tycoon Donald Trump, gave praise and a prize to Mr Autrey.[1] The film industry doesn't normally handle compassion and heroically selfless acts. The usual plotlines prefer the rags-to-riches stories of men and women who work their way out of the gutter to make something of their lives. From films like *Rocky* and *The Pursuit of Happyness* to *Pretty Woman* and *Cinderella*, we love to celebrate the well-worn journey from squalor to honour. Yet what happened on the 137th Street platform in New York demonstrated a completely different journey. Countering the survival-of-the-fittest mindset, safety was exchanged for clear and present danger; riches for rags. Wesley was prepared to risk dying for the possibility of saving someone he had never met before.

 ## Stuart

Another platform. Another country. *Stuart: A Life Backwards*, one of the most disturbing biographies I have ever read, begins on an Underground platform in London. Stuart, aged 34, sees the oncoming train and dives in front of it. Not to save another person's life, but to end his own. The book then works backwards. It starts at the end of Stuart's life and ends at the beginning, exploring the series of unfortunate events that led to this desperate end. The suicide can be understood only in the light of Stuart's tragic journey through neglect, abuse, addiction, destitution, imprisonment and betrayal.

These two true stories show the entire scope of the human dilemma. Some people find life so valuable they are willing to lay down their own lives to save another's. Others find life so empty that they can see no point in continuing theirs any longer. The Algerian existentialist philosopher Albert Camus argued that the ultimate question that philosophy had to answer was: 'Why not commit suicide?'[2] What makes life worth living? What is worth dying for?

## Me

I have been wrestling with these questions since I was a teenager. Growing up in a multicultural family with a mix of religious influences, I could never go with the flow where philosophy and religion were concerned. My mother used to read me Bible stories at bedtime and my grandmother used to take to me to Hindu temples in my holidays. I happily went to church, but was equally at home ringing the bell and prostrating myself in front of various deities. Then I saw a dramatic lifeswap in the chemistry lab of my comprehensive school.

While most of the boys were taking advantage of the form tutor's cigarette break to perform various rogue and hazardous chemical experiments, one of the quieter lads in the class stood up and told us he had become a Christian. As if that were not bizarre enough, the fact that he then proceeded to take the inevitable mockery with a calm confidence was extremely unnerving. This lad had changed.

I had to get to the bottom of this. Surely religion was cultural, the Bible was made up, Jesus was just a man, and science was on my side? And surely life was too short to bother with these questions anyway? Amazingly, I began to find out that there were some pretty convincing answers out there. But there was more.

My parents had invested a lot of energy in helping me do my best at school, and I was a good student. I needed to be, because, as one of a handful of non-white kids in a large school, I felt it was the only way I could earn respect. Even that respect was severely limited; it never prevented the name calling and breaktime bullying.

As I tried to find out how the Christian faith had turned my mate's life upside down, I discovered that Christianity was not just an interesting life philosophy or a challenging moral code. I discovered that at the centre of Christianity was the person of Jesus. Everything hinged on him. All the big ideas of the faith were dependent on who Jesus was and what he did. And this Jesus was marginalized and persecuted, and betrayed by his so-called friends. Jesus was someone I could relate to. And the more I read about him, the more I became convinced that Jesus was more than just a man. Eventually I was convinced that Jesus really was God and really had the ability to change my life.

There is no doubt that people around the world from all sorts of backgrounds or religions have a huge amount of respect for Jesus. Here is someone who at every turn was compassionate, kind, generous and courageous. He was never too busy or proud to hang out with broken people, for all the abuse he got for it. He sought out the outcast and the rejected and empowered them through his offer of forgiveness and acceptance. Although he lived two thousand years ago, he offered a way of transforming messy and mundane existence into authentic life. Everyone Jesus met in the first century was profoundly affected, and all through this book we will see people from a cross-section of society transformed: a religious expert, an excluded woman, a blind beggar, a dead man, a criminal on death row and a failed fisherman. Through these encounters we will discover what it was that made such an incredible impact and find out whether these lifeswaps are still available today.

Here is someone who at every turn was compassionate, kind, generous and courageous. He was never too busy or proud to hang out with broken people, for all the abuse he got for it. He sought out the outcast and the rejected and empowered them through his offer of forgiveness and acceptance.

Before we read how Jesus helped people swap ordinary existence for extraordinary life, we should first understand who Jesus claimed to be. The best place to start is to explore the lifeswap that Jesus himself underwent.

 **Jesus**

I know men and I tell you that Jesus Christ is no mere man. Between him and every other person in the world there is no possible term of comparison. Alexander, Caesar, Charlemagne, and I founded empires. But on what did we rest the creations of our genius? Upon force. Jesus Christ founded His empire upon love; and at this hour millions of people would die for Him... Everything in Christ astonishes me. His spirit overawes me, and His will confounds me... I search in vain in history to find the similar to Jesus Christ, or anything that can approach the gospel.[3]

There's never been anyone quite like Jesus. He stands alone in the pages of human history. His life was so significant that even our dating system is based around his birth. He has more pages devoted to him in the *Encyclopaedia Britannica* than any other person living or dead. His name is used in worship by those who believe and in profanity by those who don't. There is no question that he is at least worth some serious investigation at some point in our lives.

Although ancient Roman and Jewish historians refer to Jesus, most of our information about Jesus' life and claims is found in the Bible. The first four books of the New Testament are written by biographers Matthew, Mark, Luke and John, and they named their accounts of Jesus' life 'Gospels', which literally means 'Good News'. That is a big hint that there is something important about the life of Jesus. One of the biographers seems to be as fascinated with the lifeswap element as I am. John loves to tell stories of encounters with Jesus and to show the life-changing effect they had. He is constantly alluding to swaps. Jesus turns water into wine, funerals into celebrations, professors into students and enemies into friends.

If it seems strange that Stuart's biographer felt it necessary to start the story with the account of how Stuart ended it all, Jesus' biographer decided to start at an even more unusual point. John was a close friend of Jesus and had spent three years on the road with him. He had seen Jesus hungry, thirsty, tired, destitute, grieving, celebrating and angry. Yet the place where John wants to start his biography is not at the manger in Bethlehem, where Jesus was born, or by the lake, where John first met Jesus, or even at the cross where Jesus died, but at the beginning of time.

Although most biographies go from birth to death, there is a growing recognition in our society that the questions of identity need to start much further back. The BBC have helped some celebrities to trace their ancestries back through their family trees in a popular TV series, *Who Do You Think You Are?* As racial integration becomes more and more complex in families, there is also a recognized need to preserve heritage, languages and cultures. There is great debate regarding the origins of the universe and its impact on our understanding of our own heritage and identity. John, writing two thousand years ago, understood that individual life stories make sense only within the bigger narrative of the universe itself. John dares to claim that the beginning of the universe is intimately bound up with the identity of Jesus.

**//** In the beginning was the Word, and the Word was with God, and the Word was God. He was with God in the beginning.

Through him all things were made; without him nothing was made that has been made. In him was life, and that life was the light of men. The light shines in the darkness, but the darkness has not understood it.

There came a man who was sent from God; his name was John. He came as a witness to testify concerning that light, so that through him all men might believe. He himself was not the light; he came only as a witness to the light. The true light that gives light to every man was coming into the world.

He was in the world, and though the world was made through him, the world did not recognise him. He came to that which was his own, but his own did not receive him. Yet to all who received him, to those who believed in his name, he gave the right to become children of God – children born not of natural descent, nor of human decision or a husband's will, but born of God. The Word became flesh and made his dwelling among us. We have seen his glory, the glory of the One and Only, who came from the Father, full of grace and truth. **//** (John 1:1–14)

The first sentence of the Bible contains some of the most famous words in history: 'In the beginning God created the heavens and the earth...' They kick off the book of Genesis, which literally means 'beginning' or 'origin'. But John dares to start his biography of Jesus' life in a similarly grandiose way: 'In the beginning was the Word...'

To his original readers, John's introduction would have sounded like a stolen riff from a well-known rock song. His opening lyric is dramatic yet mysterious. For someone about to tell some fascinating stories of intimate encounters, this borrowed philosophical and grand-scale opening sentence may seem out of place. But the whole basis of John's book is a jaw-dropping revelation. A baby born in a backyard two thousand years ago is the one through whom the universe came into being. The man who walked and talked with the losers and misfits of his day is God's communication to the world. The convicted criminal who ended up dying on a cross is the same person who commanded the stars to shine at the beginning of time.

In the opening paragraphs of his biography John claims that Jesus existed before he was born in Bethlehem. In fact, he claims Jesus existed before anyone was born anywhere. John calls Jesus 'The Word', which is an ingenious redefinition of a Greek philosophical term that implied the organizing principle behind the universe. This title would also have reminded a Jewish audience of the fact that when God created the universe all he did was speak, and the stuff of the universe was created out of nothing.

John has definitely got our attention sufficiently to reveal to us in a nutshell the outrageous bombshell that Jesus is the reason for everything.

**What if Jesus is not just some interesting ancient celebrity?**

John's introduction challenges our preconceptions of Jesus, as it did those of his first-century readers. What if Jesus is not just some interesting ancient celebrity? What if he is not just some religious teacher with some great stories or soundbites? What if he is not some sage-like guru who made some challenging social observations? John wants to introduce Jesus as God himself.

He knew all that,
and yet he
chose to
be born. He
chose
to be one of us.
He
swapped safety
for insecurity.
He swapped
eternal bliss
for physical
pain.

Best known as the author of the Narnia series, the Oxford professor C.S. Lewis explained that we are left with only three choices when it comes to Jesus. Option One: Jesus was an insane lunatic. He believed he was God but he wasn't. He may as well have claimed to be a fruit smoothie as to be God himself; either way, the claims are normally qualifications for entry to asylums for the insane. Option Two: Jesus knew he wasn't God but claimed he was anyway. This makes Jesus the biggest con man in history, fooling millions of people over a period of 21 centuries. Option Three: Jesus is who he claimed to be – God walking around in human flesh. Lewis challenged people to decide – lunatic, liar or Lord? Whichever option you choose, there is no room for the most commonly held view – that Jesus was just a good, or very good man. Deciding what we do with Jesus' claim to be God is critical to our whole view of life.

Whilst reorganizing our minds to accommodate the possibility that our picture of Jesus is too small, John makes sure that we expand our picture of God, too. God is not just one person living alone on a cloud. He is a community. John introduces us first to the idea that Jesus is God, then later on in the book to God the Father, and later on again to God the Holy Spirit. One God, three persons; or what Christians refer to as the Trinity. Not three gods. Not one God with three roles. But instead, a God who is one being and yet three persons. There are no analogies that can make this concept easier to understand. The most distinguished theologians find it difficult to elucidate. Not surprisingly, God is bigger than our limited mental capacity. But the picture of God in community will prove to be key to John's descriptions of Jesus, showing God in life-changing relationship with ordinary people.

John could have told the dramatic stories that come later in his book without this initial introduction and comment. But the lifeswaps that occur throughout the book really make sense only if we understand that John is telling the first lifeswap story in the very first chapter. Jesus, just by being born, is undergoing a lifeswap beyond imagination or compare.

John claims that Jesus is God and existed before time in heaven, in the bliss of eternal perfection and community. Then Jesus chose to swap his life of glory to become human. Not just human, but Jewish human. Not just Jewish human, but at a time when Israel was occupied by the Romans, under an oppressive and corrupt regime. Jesus becomes not just an oppressed Jewish human but a poverty-stricken marginalized-northern oppressed Jewish human. When God chose to become man, he dived down from the heights of heaven to the lowest of the low points in human history and geography to do it.

In Shakespeare's *Henry V* there is a key moment just before the crucial battle scene. It is 25 October 1415, and Henry's English troops are poised to take on Charles VI's French forces. On the eve of the battle, we see the outnumbered English forces encamped on French soil, and we can imagine the tension in the camp. Shakespeare describes how King Henry, under cover of darkness, walks among his men dressed as a common soldier. He listens to his men as an equal and speaks words of courage to prepare them for the battle ahead. Shakespeare's picture of a humble king among his people could have been inspired by John's account of Jesus. John draws a similar picture, of God himself walking among his people as one of us.

For John's Jewish readers this was not going to be easy to swallow. Their scriptures were full of extreme examples of how dangerous God's presence was. Even a glimpse of God was like staring into the sun. Some would die; others would fall on their knees. They had to protect themselves by following God's guidelines closely and needed rituals, priests and thick temple walls to shield themselves. Their scriptures were also full of high-profile trailblazers: Abraham, Moses, David. They had no reason to expect God's promised messenger to be any less visible or any less glorious.

When Jesus came to earth he came in under the radar. Low profile. He hid the full extent of his glory from us, so that he could relate to us as equals. Jesus swapped glory for ignominy. Jesus swapped the honour of the Son of God for the disrepute of being known as the son of a northern Jewish carpenter. Jesus swapped the power of being the ruler of the universe for the life of a man with no political power, no financial resources and no preferential treatment.

Before my children were born. I had made sure that my route to the hospital was memorized. I had worked out which route to take if the baby was coming in the morning and which way to go if it was the middle of the night. Traffic lights, congestion, distances, alternative routes had all been taken into account in meticulous detail. Whatever happened, nothing was going to stop me ensuring that my baby was going to be born in the confines of a pristine, hygienic, well-staffed local hospital.

Jesus' birth was even more meticulously planned: in fact hundreds of years earlier the Old Testament prophets made it very clear where God was planning for his son to be born and under what circumstances. But God was not planning the majesty of a royal palace, or the safety of a twenty-first-century hospital. Instead, God chose for his son to be born in an occupied territory, among the poor, in the squalor of a borrowed stable. God chose a manger on that first Christmas.

The manger tells us that God understands. The manger tells us that God is humble. The manger tells us that God is with us. God is not some ivory-tower deity untouched by human pain and misery. Right from the moment of his birth, Jesus identified with the weak, the rejected, the outcast, downtrodden and penniless. Jesus experienced human life in all its grim reality.

**The manger tells us that God understands. The manger tells us that God is humble. The manger tells us that God is with us.**

When I dropped my daughter off on her first day of school, my own school years flashed past my eyes. I suddenly recalled, as if it were yesterday, the awkward feeling of walking into a whole classroom full of strangers. I remembered the cruel playground pranks. The stress of trying to fit in. The fear of getting picked last for sports teams. The panic of homework and essay deadlines. The laborious laboratories. The long nights cramming for exams. What a relief, I felt, that it was all behind me. There was no way I would ever choose to go through all that again. I was very glad my daughter had no clue about the rollercoaster ride ahead of her.

God knew exactly what he was getting into when he became human. He knew what it was going to be like to be a defenceless baby. He knew what it was going to feel like to be a frustrated toddler. He knew the challenges of adolescence. He knew he would face the pain of being a single man in a culture that really valued only married people with heirs. He knew what it was going to feel like to be betrayed by friends; to be falsely accused and then mercilessly beaten and crucified. He knew all that, and yet he chose to be born. He chose to be one of us. He swapped safety for insecurity. He swapped eternal bliss for physical pain.

This lifeswap of Jesus, swapping Paradise for Palestine, was not a social experiment. It had a purpose. John is very keen to tell us at the beginning of the book that Jesus came to offer everyone 'the right to become children of God'. In other words, because of Jesus' ultimate lifeswap, lifeswaps are available to all of us.

My favorite Eddie Murphy movie is the classic 1980s comedy *Trading Places*. Two successful stockbrokers, Mortimer and Randolph Duke, take a bet. Randolph wagers that he can take a criminal from the gutter and turn him into a high-flying business man. Eddie Murphy plays the lowlife Billy Ray, who is taken from the street. He is given the life of Louis – a high-flying yuppie who has charges fabricated against him and ends up destitute. The swap is made – one man's life for another. One person gets glory, the other humiliation. This is a rags-to-riches story at the expense of another person's riches-to-rags story. The exchange that takes place in this film reminds me of the great exchange that takes place in the opening chapter of John's Gospel. Jesus goes from heaven to earth: not because he was made to, but because he chose to. Jesus goes from heaven to earth: but not to offer just one person the status he left behind, but to offer everyone the same status of being adopted into God's family.

This was yet another hard-to-swallow jagged little pill of truth for many of John's first readers. Many Jewish people thought that they had an automatic right to claim God as their Father. But John is clear that the qualifying factors have nothing to do with upbringing, culture or family tradition. In fact, this message is just as challenging today. Many of us rely on the fact that we live in a so-called 'Christian country', have a certificate of christening or have attended religious education classes at school to provide us with a right to pray when we are in real trouble and a pass to heaven when we die.

John has challenged us about our view of Jesus and our understanding of God. Now he wants us to have a radical reorientation of our understanding of Christianity. Growing up, I perceived Christianity as a load of religious rules, restrictions and rituals. I thought it was an exclusive club for people who had some kind of deficiency or emotional vacuum in their lives. But what John claims is something far more drastic. Christianity is not about where you spend a Sunday morning. It is not a bolt-on extra in life for those who want a spiritual pick-me-up. Christianity is about enjoying the intimacy of being adopted into God's family, and it all revolves around how we have responded to Jesus.

I wonder what was going through Cameron's mind when he fell into the path of the oncoming train. I wonder if he had given up hope of rescue. Surely nobody in their right mind would risk their life for his. What was going through Stuart's mind as he fell into the path of the oncoming train? I wonder if he had given up hope of rescue. Surely nobody would adopt him into an unconditionally loving family? Jesus became like us to give us hope of an entirely new dimension to life.

Jesus became like us so that we could become like him. People around the world have been so inspired by Jesus' humility and compassion that they have left good jobs, nice homes and safe cities and towns to go and work amongst the poorest of the poor in shanty towns, slums and favelas. I have seen a university professor get on his hands and knees and help clean the carpet after old-age pensioners, because he wanted to be like Jesus. I have seen a successful chief executive give up his annual leave to help out on a children's camp, because he wanted to be like Jesus.

John's introduction is this: when Jesus became like us, God became flesh. When we look at Jesus, we see God. When we believe Jesus, we become part of his family. When we become part of his family, we seek to become like Jesus. This is such mind-blowing information that it is hard to take in. It's like a trailer for a movie that compresses 90 minutes of action into 90 seconds. They whet our appetite to see how these themes are going to be played out within the rest of the book.

God became flesh. And this is just the beginning. Once we have begun to get our heads around the enormity of this fact and its consequences for the world and for us, we begin to see that any personal encounter with Jesus is unlikely to be like any other chance meeting. This is why the stories of the people in the chapters that follow have stood the test of time – intriguing and inspiring people for thousands of years, causing people in their millions to ask for the same lifeswap from Jesus for themselves.

### Notes

1. http://news.bbc.co.uk/1/hi/world/americas/6231971.stm

2. Albert Camus, *The Myth of Sisyphus and Other Essays*, translated by Justin O'Brien, London: Hamish Hamilton, 1955, p. 11.

3. Napoleon Bonaparte, cited in Vernon C. Grounds, *The Reason for Our Hope*, Chicago: Moody Press, p. 37, cited in Josh McDowell, *Evidence that Demands a Verdict*, Scripture Press, 1990, p. 106.

# click

I'm sure it's too late
for a fresh start!

oi was a stunning brunette; she was toned and tanned. She was a successful property developer with her own dream home to match. She had a vast network of friends from around the world. They would often visit just to chat and admire her artwork and interior designs. Her lover was equally desirable and fulfilled her every fantasy. Gorgeous, popular, happy, successful...

At a computer somewhere on the not-so-virtual side of cyberspace sits a slightly overweight divorcee at a desk strewn with paperwork, apple cores and chocolate wrappers. Under stress from long working hours, financial pressures and the complications of friends choosing between her and her ex, her lifeline is Second Life, where with a click of the mouse she can become Joi every night. No hassle. No cost. No pain. No questions asked. This is the virtual world of Second Life, where all your dreams can come true. You can change your face, your waist, your bust, your income, your gender. You can create the life you always wanted.

Second Life. It doesn't only happen online. A businessman can exchange his suit for a football shirt, his empty office for a crowded stadium, and he takes on a whole new persona. A busy parent can shut the door on the cluttered bedrooms and demanding teenagers and sit with a book in the coffee shop on the other side of town and feel like a different person.

Second Life. The less well-off dream about it as they buy their lottery tickets. The more well-off demand it as they buy their place in the sun. The sick pray for it as the results of the tests come back. The healthy pay for it as they go under the knife of the plastic surgeon. As we read our magazines and novels, as we shop, or as we sip coffee at our neighbour's table, as we attend weddings and funerals, we try to imagine ourselves in other people's shoes.

Second Life. Jesus knew that human nature would always crave a new identity, a new spouse, a new body, a new job, a new challenge. John's biography of Jesus is careful to include how Jesus delivers a series of radical transformations which point us to Jesus' ultimate offer of a second life for us all.

 ## Second wind

Take John's record of Jesus' first miracle. Jesus is at a party, enjoying the company of the guests and the celebration of a new marriage. But the atmosphere is changing: the buzz is cooling off, the guests are getting restless, and the host is having a domestic crisis. Jesus gives that party second wind by replenishing the dwindling supplies at the bar. He takes ordinary water and turns it into extraordinary wine.

This miracle does not square with many people's image of Jesus. They would be more comfortable if he had taken wine and changed it into water. After all, many people see God as a cosmic spoilsport who struggles with the possibility that somewhere someone could be having some fun. But the first miracle that Jesus performs blows these preconceptions and sets the agenda for the rest of his life.

Jesus saves the embarrassment of a host who has failed to provide enough wine for his son's wedding. Jesus doesn't step in to destroy the party, but to enhance it. And how he does it gives us a clue to his mission. Jesus takes the enormous water holders that were used in the religious washing ceremonies and transforms their contents into the best party wine the guests have ever tasted. Jesus is going to turn the religious practice of his day upside down and transform it into a life-affirming, God-centred celebration.

 ## Second place

What happens next? Jesus goes into the Jerusalem temple to find it full of traders arguing noisily as they exchanged currencies. His fellow Jews had come with Roman currency to change so they could pay their temple dues. This perfectly legitimate exchange programme was offering a helpful service to the worshippers. The problem was where and how it was happening. The only place in the temple where a non-Jewish person could pray was now full of the hustle and bustle of a roaring trade. Our preconceptions are again blown out of the water, as the traders are thrown out of the temple not by 'gentle Jesus, meek and mild', but by an angry Jesus, enraged and incensed. He knew that he needed to put the traders in their place by physically driving them out of the temple courts, overturning the tables. Jesus, an out-of-towner, is headlined in the local news as the one who cried out 'This is to be a place of prayer for all nations....'

Non-Jews were not second class in Jesus' eyes. Jesus made sure they were not in second place. He made sure there was space for them. Again he challenges the accepted religious practice. As the story unfolds we will see just how far Jesus is willing to go to provide accessibility to the presence of God.

## Second chance

We have seen Jesus turn religious water into party wine, and a place of business into a place of prayer. What happens next is a radical lifeswap.

**//** Now there was a man of the Pharisees named Nicodemus, a member of the Jewish ruling council. He came to Jesus at night and said, 'Rabbi, we know you are a teacher who has come from God. For no one could perform the miraculous signs you are doing if God were not with him.'

In reply Jesus declared, 'I tell you the truth, no one can see the kingdom of God unless he is born again.'

'How can a man be born when he is old?' Nicodemus asked. 'Surely he cannot enter a second time into his mother's womb to be born!'

Jesus answered, 'I tell you the truth, no one can enter the kingdom of God unless he is born of water and the Spirit. Flesh gives birth to flesh, but the Spirit gives birth to spirit. You should not be surprised at my saying, "You must be born again." The wind blows wherever it pleases. You hear its sound, but you cannot tell where it comes from or where it is going. So it is with everyone born of the Spirit.'

'How can this be?' Nicodemus asked.

'You are Israel's teacher,' said Jesus, 'and do you not understand these things? I tell you the truth, we speak of what we know, and we testify to what we have seen, but still you people do not accept our testimony. I have spoken to you of earthly things and you do not believe; how then will you believe if I speak of heavenly things? No one has ever gone into heaven except the one who came from heaven – the Son of Man. Just as Moses lifted up the snake in the desert, so the Son of Man must be lifted up, that everyone who believes in him may have eternal life.

'For God so loved the world that he gave his one and only Son, that whoever believes in him shall not perish but have eternal life. For God did not send his Son into the world to condemn the world, but to save the world through him. Whoever believes in him is not condemned, but whoever does not believe stands condemned already because he has not believed in the name of God's one and only Son. This is the verdict: Light has come into the world, but men loved darkness instead of light because their deeds were evil. Everyone who does evil hates the light, and will not come into the light for fear that his deeds will be exposed. But whoever lives by the truth comes into the light, so that it may be seen plainly that what he has done has been done through God.' // (John 3:1–21)

Under the cover of darkness, Nicodemus, a high-profile religious leader, comes to visit Jesus. He was a politician, an academic and a cleric, and at that time those accolades won him the trust and respect of his community. Yet he comes at night. Perhaps he was avoiding the first-century paparazzi. Perhaps his daytime schedule was too heavy. Perhaps the darkness was symbolic of Nicodemus' imminent lifeswap, as lights get switched on during his life-changing encounter with Jesus of Nazareth.

Nicodemus begins with a surprisingly humble greeting. The old man with the grey beard and all the theological qualifications you could need addresses the fresh-faced young man with a woodwork apprenticeship: 'Teacher, Rabbi'. The words are a compliment, a sign of respect, and part of his pre-planned spiel, which continues:

'we know you are a teacher sent by God, for no one could do the things you have done without some power devolved by God himself.' A spiel maybe, but respectful, humble, conciliatory, gracious and hopeful.

I would be flattered to have someone come to me like this, even if it were in the middle of the night. It would be like hosting Sir Right Reverend Bishop Professor Lord Knowall, who usually travelled with an entourage and a limo. Here was a photo-opportunity and a half. Here was a chance to get in with the right crowd. Here was a chance to win the backing of a major national player.

How would Jesus react? What would Jesus say? Not to be second-guessed, Jesus cuts through all the niceties and tells Nicodemus plainly he needs a second life.

 ## Second opinion

My mum knew something was wrong when she shook the doctor's hand. He held on just a little too long. Then he told her to sit down. He asked the nurse to fetch my father. He struggled for words and then started his sentence with the words, 'I'm really sorry.' My mum didn't really remember much of that conversation: the information about the type of cancer it was; why they didn't spot it earlier; what the prognosis was. She didn't need a second opinion – it all made sense. She heard the words 'cancer' and 'I'm sorry', and the world suddenly seemed to turn upside down. Bad news changes everything.

When Nicodemus heard the words 'I tell you the truth, no one can see the kingdom of God unless he is born again,' it was bad news. He knew that something was wrong

– something just didn't click and he was hoping that Jesus would be able to solve the problem. But this bad news meant that everything he had lived for was turned upside down. He needed more than a vitamin boost, more than a course of antibiotics, more than major surgery – he needed a whole life transplant. He tried to make an awkward joke, as we do when we are so taken aback we can't think of anything sensible to say. But imagining climbing back into his mother's womb for a second shot at life did not detract from his growing realization that this was serious.

 ## Bad news

If this was bad news for the respected theologian-in-residence, what chance did anybody else stand? This statement would have floored most of the original audience of John's biography of Jesus. If the most respected religious expert of their community wasn't anywhere near good enough for God, everyone else was in deep trouble. If Nicodemus wasn't accepted for automatic entry to the kingdom of God, then nobody else stood a chance in hell.

The kingdom of God was what the Jews had been desperately longing for: God back in control instead of the oppressive Roman Empire. We can relate to them. When we switch on the television news and see the horrors from around the globe, it feels like either God isn't doing a good job, or he has taken a leave of absence. We long for him to put it all right. The Bible is very clear that God is the Creator of the universe, and that he actually claims sovereignty over every atom of it. The Bible is also clear that the reason there are suffering, injustice, poverty and disasters is not because God is a bad ruler, but because of our decision as humankind to go it alone. When the

Jewish nation ignored God's guidelines, the whole sorry story was prophesied and recorded in the Old Testament: its rebellion, the invasion, exile and return to Israel. And there was one more prophecy – the promise that God would institute a revolution and establish his kingdom through his chosen King, the Messiah. The Jews desperately expected this Messiah to oust the Romans in the process. Jesus' own words seemed to confirm this in the world's most famous prayer, the one he taught his disciples: 'Your kingdom come on earth as it is in heaven'.

So when Jesus told a high-ranking Jewish leader that he was not fit to see the kingdom of God, it implied he was not good enough either to see God's revolution begin on earth or to experience heaven. Anyone who overheard that conversation would have been shocked. If Nicodemus, with all his strict observance of the religious laws of his faith, with all of his public good works, with all his moral high ground, was not ready for heaven on earth nor heaven after death, then heaven help the rest of us.

Most of us believe that by being good, law-abiding citizens, good, thoughtful neighbours and good supporters of local causes, we stand a chance if we ever were to meet God. But when Jesus tells a professional that his religious observance isn't enough, then the bar is raised beyond achievable limits for all of us. Even good isn't good enough.

Imagine I get round to taking my new(ish), well-looked-after car to a local garage to fix an oil leak. The mechanic makes a sharp intake of breath, in a way that only mechanics know how. He puts his hand on my shoulder and tells me I need a brand-new car. There is nothing I or he can do. There is no simple tweak he can perform, no screw that can be tightened and no part that can be replaced. He tells me my car is

He needed more than a vitamin boost, more than a course of antibiotics, more than major surgery — he needed a whole life transplant.

a write-off and there's no option but to cut my losses and get a replacement. Jesus presents Nicodemus with the same verdict. There is no tweak that can be performed on his life; he can't be fixed with just a few more good deeds, a pilgrimage, or more regular attendance at religious services. His life is a write-off. He needs a whole new second life.

It might be the kind of verdict we would expect for some people. But Jesus is not issuing this harsh warning to a mass murderer, a serial rapist or a people trafficker. Jesus is telling an upstanding beyond-reproach member of society, a religiously zealous and probably theologically orthodox man that his life, and therefore all life, is a complete write-off.

 ## The good news

Another write-off. Not a new(ish) well-looked-after car, but a second-hand second-time-around-the-clock car. Stumbling out of the wreck, at the traffic lights. The once smooth lines now jagged. Fluid all over the floor. The van whose fault it was annoyingly unscathed. Thankfully, no one had been hurt. The only victim – my car – was now a large piece of unwanted scrap metal sitting in the middle of the crossroads. The witnesses corroborated my story that I had had the right of way. The police signed off that I was in the right. And when I had calmed down from the shock of the accident, I realized that the bad news actually meant good news. The sticky clutch was not going to be a problem any more. The dodgy passenger seat would never annoy me again. The patch of rust under the wheel arch would not need to be dealt with. The old car was gone and, thanks to my insurers, a new one was on its way.

Jesus' disarming pronouncement that Nicodemus needed a second life is actually an incredible promise of a second chance. All of us, from the Nicodemuses of this world downwards, are at one fell swoop pronounced a write-off, but with the same fell swoop offered a fresh start.

A fresh start reminds me of school exercise books. Most of us have a handful of them somewhere in somebody's loft, covered in ink-stains and doodles, dog-eared and dog-chewed. Red pen marks with more crosses than you thought were possible, and still smelling of apple cores and pencil sharpenings from your desk. They all end up with the same fate, no matter how neat our handwriting, or how hard we tried. What a relief it was, on the first day of each autumn term, when the teacher handed out the new exercise books. The feel of the pristine pages, the smell of the fresh paper. They inspired in all of us the resolution of a new start – with neater than neat handwriting, Da Vinci-style illustrations and As on every page. Of course, this fresh start never lived up to the promise. Three weeks into term and they were already a literal write-off. But those fresh pages did feel good for a while.

We all dream of fresh starts, whether it is a new term at school, a new car, a new kitchen or a new life, and most solutions are disappointingly temporary. Jesus' solution of a completely new second life offers more: a radical, permanent, satisfying chance to lifeswap into his kingdom.

So how does it work? If our lives are so damaged because of our rebellion against God that they can't be fixed by a bit of hard work, good deeds, or willpower, how is it possible that Jesus is able to offer this new start? Is it too good to be true?

Nicodemus certainly found the suggestion incredible. But then Jesus also found it incredible that, even though Nicodemus was so well versed in the Old Testament, he had missed its point. Jesus patiently and succinctly began to click some lights on for Nicodemus. His argument is simple. He explains the two births as physical and spiritual. He likens the spiritual dimension to the wind, which cannot be seen or controlled, but can be heard and sensed. And then he uses an image from Nicodemus' own specialist subject: the Old Testament.

**//** '**Just as Moses lifted up the snake in the desert, so the Son of Man must be lifted up, that everyone who believes in him may have eternal life.**' **//**
(John 3:15)

Nicodemus did not need to be reminded of who Moses was – the great hero of the Jewish nation, who rescued them from slavery to the Egyptians and brought them through the desert to the Promised Land. He did not need to be reminded of the history of how the hard-hearted Pharoah of Egypt had not wanted to lose his free slave labour and had pursued the fleeing Jews, but how his military superpower was defeated by a defenceless nation and its God. He did not need to be reminded of the accounts of the long slog through the desert, which made everyone complain that even Egypt with its meat, veg and torture had been a breeze in comparison. He did not need to be reminded of the context of the snake episode, when many of the travellers were bitten, poisoned and killed, and how God had responded to Moses' pleas for help by commanding him to lift a bronze snake up on a pole for people to look up to for healing and rescue. He did not need to be reminded of the significance that a gracious God was offering his moody, rebellious people a second chance at life. But Nicodemus did need Jesus to teach him the further significance of this Old Testament story with which he was so familiar. Jesus explained that the Son of Man (a title he applied to himself) was also going to be lifted up to provide healing, rescue and a second chance at life. Jesus was talking about his future death on the cross, when his body was literally lifted up from the ground on a stake.

And then, knowing that Nicodemus could not have imagined such a powerful prophecy staring him in the face in one of his best-studied stories, Jesus spells it out, in one of the most famous verses in the Bible. This verse captures the Christian message:

> // // 'For God so loved the world that he gave his one and only Son, that whoever believes in him shall not perish but have eternal life.' // //
> (John 3:16)

Although Jesus has used a well-known story from Jewish history, he now clearly informs Nicodemus that God is not a tribal deity, interested in only one people or nation. God's love extends to all people, from the religious elite to the social dropouts. God is not partisan, racist, homophobic, sexist or snobbish. Jesus makes the categorical statement that God loves the whole world.

And this divine love is not a mere sentimental feeling: it leads to costly sacrifice. What parent wouldn't willingly give anything and everything to keep their children safe from harm? But God's sacrifice is, strangely, not *for* his one and only son, but *of* his one and only son. Just as the bronze snake raised in the desert was the only way the Jewish nation could be rescued, the Son of God lifted on the cross was the only way the life-threatening sins of the world could be dealt with.

Here is the ultimate lifeswap. Jesus died on the cross in order that we could escape death and have life. The Son of God chose to give up his life and face death. This is such a central theme in John's account of Jesus' life that we will be exploring it again in later chapters. But at this point the key idea is the willing swap of God's own perfect life for our write-off of a life, which is the only way that we can get a real second life.

Imagine being in trouble with the law. You end up convicted by a court for your crimes and it is time for sentencing. You know that the sentence is going to be severe, but entirely appropriate for your crimes. You know you are guilty and the court knows you are guilty. There are no excuses, no extenuating circumstances, no chance of running or buying your way out of trouble. You are offered the chance to speak, and knowing you are completely defenceless, in utter desperation you express your heartfelt regret for what you have done. You confess that you don't deserve anything from the judge but you ask for mercy.

The judge turns to you. You can see his outrage at your crime. You can also see his compassion. He takes out a piece of paper with your sentence on it, picks up his pen, crosses out your name and inserts his own. He tells you that you are free to go, as he steps down from his bench, hands himself over to the bailiff, and is dragged away to face your punishment.

This is a picture of God, who sits in heaven with the right to judge the world, but steps down into the world offering to take the punishment for humanity's crimes. The opportunity of a second chance and a fresh start is available to all, according to Jesus, and is conditional only on looking in faith on the death of Jesus, trusting him for access to this unconditional love and this incredibly costly gift of a second life.

When Nicodemus, an expert in all things religious, came to Jesus, he came humbly to ask about access to the kingdom of heaven. Jesus' credentials as a fresh-faced carpenter's apprentice from Nazareth may have seemed weak. Why did Nicodemus accept what Jesus had to say?

What if I were to tell you about a place where, in order to get into the loft, you have first to find the second smallest bedroom, where in the wardrobe is a pole with a hook on it and a stool that is hiding below a pile of unironed clothes? Take both these tools and, in the correct order, unlatch the two bolt locks, twist the catch lock and make sure you have a strong hand to catch the falling ladder. Also make sure your mouth is closed, because, as the door opens, it is highly likely that a certain amount of dust will fall straight into your face. Now there is probably not a reader out there who could challenge my description or instructions. The loft is in my house, and I am uniquely qualified to tell you authoritatively how to access it.

Nicodemus accepted Jesus' authority on the subject of heaven because Jesus came from heaven. No one had ever done that, before or since. He is uniquely qualified and so his words can be taken seriously.

At the beginning of this chapter, we saw Jesus authorize access to God's presence for non-Jews by clearing away the religious double standards of the money changers. Now, at the end of the chapter, we see Jesus authorize access to God's presence for the whole world by offering his own life as a swap for ours.

## Lifeswap – the aftermath

In the movie *Click*, Michael Newman finds himself literally fast-forwarding through life with a 'universal' remote control. Because he is a workaholic, the remote control begins to automatically fast-forward him through his home life and his family life. Before he knows it, he is an old man, feeling that he has missed out on something. Like Nicodemus he is powerful and successful, and something just does not feel right. Michael eventually returns to where he started, having learned lessons from his encounter with the God-figure in the film. So what happens to Nicodemus?

**//** Later, Joseph of Arimathea asked Pilate for the body of Jesus. Now Joseph was a disciple of Jesus, but secretly because he feared the Jews. With Pilate's permission, he came and took the body away. He was accompanied by Nicodemus, the man who earlier had visited Jesus at night. Nicodemus brought a mixture of myrrh and aloes, about seventy-five pounds. Taking Jesus' body, the two of them wrapped it, with the spices, in strips of linen. This was in accordance with Jewish burial customs. **//**
(John 19:38–40)

Nicodemus' life was transformed the day he met Jesus. He came at night, afraid of what his disapproving fellow Pharisees might say about him. However, the next time we hear of him he is no longer afraid, despite how dangerous it had become to be associated with Jesus. A public figure, Nicodemus went public about his faith in Jesus, to the point that his own life was at risk. A rich man, Nicodemus was generous in his handling of the burial expenses. An encounter with Jesus turned a teacher into a disciple, a scared man into a brave man, a puzzled man into a man for whom the pieces of the puzzle now all clicked into place.

Nicodemus experienced a spiritual rebirth as he trusted in the death of Jesus for his own rescue into the kingdom of God. If this iconic religious guru needed to take a second look at his spiritual status, how much more the rest of us? Jesus really is offering a second chance to all of us by offering to swap his perfect life for our life write-offs. A second shot at life and a second life after death.

# quench

I've tried it all before and
nothing really works, does it?

**H**arrods at Christmas. Santa's grotto may as well have been Lapland, as far as my kids were concerned. For weeks, they had been eagerly anticipating the trip to visit the mythical figure in red and white. Each morning they groaned, as the slow countdown still hadn't reached the day of the trip. All our reassurances that their patience would pay off was pointless. But finally, after weeks of 'Is it today yet?' 'today' arrived. Everyone got up early in the morning, threw on hats and scarves for the foggy walk to the tube station and took the long, slow underground train to Knightsbridge. As we counted down the stops, it must have seemed forever to a two-and-a-half-year-old. And once we arrived, there was the queue. A gloomy sign in the menswear department indicated 'Four hours wait from this point'. Thank goodness our two-and-a-half-year-old couldn't read! Harrods staff dressed as elves helpfully came round with water, and unhelpfully with sticky lollipops with whistles for sticks.

It was a long few hours for the adults, with screeching whistles blowing from all around and sugary children pushing from all sides. But by 11 o'clock we were in the grotto, with stuffed reindeer singing through the glass display cases and a very chirpy elf directing us to one of twelve Santa rooms. Sitting on the lap of what he believed to be the one and only Father Christmas, our son was asked what he wanted for Christmas. It's the moment all parents dread. What if it is something we can't afford? What if it is something that Amazon can't deliver on time? What if he asks for a dog – or another brother?! But what our two-and-a-half-year-old asked for, after weeks of anticipation, ages spent on cold platforms and stuffy trains and in sticky queues was something born out of his bitter experience, and much harder to deliver. Out came a single word: 'Patience.'

My son's non-materialistic wish list did not last long. The following Christmas he wanted a skateboard and a beanbag. The year after that it was a bike and a Playstation. Now peer pressure, TV advertisements and catalogues through the post definitely feed his impressionable young mind and brainwash him into wanting the wish list of every seven-year-old boy in the country. Not that adults are any less affected by materialism. Most of our wish lists are similarly predictable.

 ## Thirst for more

One science fiction series featured an episode where a man wished for a new yacht. He was taken at his word, and the delivery was immediate and incredibly accurate. The yacht instantly landed on his lap, crushing him to death. The moral of the story was dramatically clear. Be careful what you wish for. The man probably had a picture in his mind of himself on his yacht at the marina, sun shining, no worries in the world, respected by passers-by, free to go where he pleased. But the things we really want in life, such as freedom, respect, love, security and warm weather, don't come from the things we own. This is why whatever we buy ends up disappointing us. We thirst after more, but more is never enough.

The animal instinct to crave more without stopping to think is horrifically illustrated in the Eskimo culture.[1] Eskimos used to trap the wolves that preyed on them by painting a razor-sharp knife with layers of blood, which instantly froze. The knife is then pushed into the ground so that the scent can be picked up. The wolf stalking through the night is drawn to the blood lollipop and, as his primal instincts take over, licks his way into a frenzy. The wolf is so consumed by his pleasure that he is not aware when the blood he is drinking stops being the blood on the knife, but that of his own mouth. In the morning, the Eskimo collects the dead wolf impaled on the knife. This barbaric and cruel means of trapping wolves could be a metaphor for our times. Uncontrollable consumption and greed is not harmless, but could contain the seeds of our own downfall and destruction. Satisfying our thirsts in life can be a dangerous pursuit.

## Thirst for happiness

Perhaps the pursuit of happiness was simpler before the age of catalogues, consoles and Christmas as we know it. The first-century search for satisfaction is where John takes us next, on his radical introduction to Jesus. He has already used some powerful illustrations to describe Jesus' transforming encounters: heaven to earth; water to wine; marketplace to prayer room; elderly professor to newborn disciple.

Jesus has just shown Nicodemus out of the door. Out goes the high-ranking, highly respected teacher of the Jewish nation. Then into the picture comes a stark contrast. John's next featured encounter is a local lowlife.

> **The Pharisees heard that Jesus was gaining and baptising more disciples than John, although in fact it was not Jesus who baptised, but his disciples. When the Lord learned of this, he left Judea and went back once more to Galilee.**

Now he had to go through Samaria. So he came to a town in Samaria called Sychar, near the plot of ground Jacob had given to his son Joseph. Jacob's well was there, and Jesus, tired as he was from the journey, sat down by the well. It was about the sixth hour. When a Samaritan woman came to draw water, Jesus said to her, 'Will you give me a drink?' (His disciples had gone into the town to buy food.)

The Samaritan woman said to him, 'You are a Jew and I am a Samaritan woman. How can you ask me for a drink?' (For Jews do not associate with Samaritans.)

Jesus answered her, 'If you knew the gift of God and who it is that asks you for a drink, you would have asked him and he would have given you living water.'

'Sir,' the woman said, 'you have nothing to draw with and the well is deep. Where can you get this living water? Are you greater than our father Jacob, who gave us the well and drank from it himself, as did also his sons and his flocks and herds?'

Jesus answered, 'Everyone who drinks this water will be thirsty again, but whoever drinks the water I give him will never thirst. Indeed, the water I give him will become in him a spring of water welling up to eternal life.'

The woman said to him, 'Sir, give me this water so that I won't get thirsty and have to keep coming here to draw water.'

He told her, 'Go, call your husband and come back.'

'I have no husband,' she replied.

Jesus said to her, 'You are right when you say you have no husband. The fact is, you have had five husbands, and the man you now have is not your husband. What you have just said is quite true.'

'Sir,' the woman said, 'I can see that you are a prophet. Our fathers worshiped on this mountain, but you Jews claim that the place where we must worship is in Jerusalem.'

Jesus declared, 'Believe me, woman, a time is coming when you will worship the Father neither on this mountain nor in Jerusalem. You Samaritans worship what you do not know; we worship what we do know, for salvation is from the Jews. Yet a time is coming and has now come when the true worshipers will worship the Father in spirit and truth, for they are the kind of worshippers the Father seeks. God is spirit, and his worshippers must worship in spirit and in truth.'

The woman said, 'I know that Messiah' (called Christ) 'is coming. When he comes, he will explain everything to us.'

Then Jesus declared, 'I who speak to you am he.' / / (John 4:1–26)

It was a hot and dusty day, and while the disciples went into town, Jesus took the opportunity for a rest. He was becoming so popular in Judea that people were queuing up to have him initiate them as his followers by baptism in the river. So, in order to find some peace and quiet, he had left town to return home to Galilee. Most Jewish people attempting this journey would have willingly travelled an extra-long detour rather than set foot in what they considered to be the God forsaken land of Samaria. Once a nation with a fine pedigree, the Samaritans had been invaded and resettled and were now considered by the Jews to be racially impure, morally suspect and religiously backward.

John provocatively states that Jesus had actually chosen to travel into Samaria and had been left alone by his disciples for a midday siesta, while they popped into town to rustle up some lunch. John's readers would have been shocked. No sensible person would go to Samaria, nor be outside in the middle of the day, under the blistering noonday sun. But this is only the beginning. Worse is to come.

At the well where Jesus chooses to rest is a lone woman. For many devout Jewish men the alarm bells would have been ringing already. Some Jewish men would use a daily prayer thanking God that he had not made them a Gentile or a woman. Women were distinctly second-class – in many cases treated worse than animals, legally and publicly demoted. Even to be seen talking with a woman alone in a public place was deemed shameful for a male Jew.

**Most Jewish people attempting this journey would have willingly travelled an extra-long detour rather than set foot in what they considered to be the God-forsaken land of Samaria.**

That this woman was visiting the well by herself at the hottest part of the day is itself strange. This woman is unacceptable. She is either avoiding the crowds or banned from polite company. We find out later that she is carrying baggage apart from the water jar. She has skeletons that have come out of the closet and follow her around. Yet John does not try to hide the fact that the Jesus who has just entertained a famous A-list celebrity now engages with a notorious X-rated divorcee. Jesus, who met a publicly upstanding man in the middle of the night, is now not afraid to meet a morally suspect woman in the middle of the day. Jesus has publicly broken two major social taboos: by entering the hated Samaritan nation and by talking to a Samaritan woman with a bad reputation.

When the audience get over the initial shock, they will be expecting Jesus to make some politically correct statement about the sanctity of the Jewish nation. But what follows is much more intimate and life-changing than they could ever have dared to imagine.

quench

**53**

The conversation starts naturally enough. Jesus asks for a drink. The woman is taken aback and questions the audacity of a Jewish man requesting help from a Samaritan woman. Then the conversation gets a little metaphysical.

But when Jesus suggests that he has access to living water, the Samaritan woman responds with an ironic remark noting that he needs his own well and also a bucket! Jesus tries again to show her that any water from any bucket from any well can quench her natural thirst only temporarily, and that there are much deeper thirsts for which he is offering permanent satisfaction.

But the woman still cannot think beyond physical water, so Jesus helps her make the connection by asking her to go and fetch her husband. The tone then changes sharply. The woman who is not afraid to question the political correctness of Jesus' request at the well, who is not afraid to tease a man who seems to be offering the impossible, and who is not afraid to put her order in for this miracle water, clams up when the subject comes too close to home.

It is Jesus' turn to be up close and personal. He reminds her that she has had five husbands and is now living with another man who is not her husband. Was Jesus trying to disarm the woman by catching her off guard on a touchy subject? Was he trying to make her feel guilty? Was he trying to prove to her that he had amazing supernatural abilities? None of these possibilities square up with the Jesus who is prepared to risk his own reputation by talking to a Samaritan woman. Jesus chooses to talk personally and privately with a multiple divorcee because there is a link in the conversation between satisfying thirst and her series of failed relationships.

She was probably a teenager when she first got married – and expected to be wed for life. But for some reason there was a breakdown of the marriage. It was virtually impossible in those days for a woman to divorce her husband, so she was probably the one abandoned and divorced. In the ancient world being single brought shame on a whole family dynasty, so the woman married again, this time with bitter experience behind her, but still hopeful that the next relationship would prove more satisfying. Again she was let down, and three more times she experiences the pain of breakdown. So when Mr Right the sixth turns up, perhaps she decides not to jinx it and goes against cultural norms by living together without getting married.

This thirst for a successful, happy, satisfying relationship is common to us all. But disappointment is not an uncommon ending. Only in fairy tales do couples marry and live happily ever after. In the real world marriage breakdown, family break-up and even broken friendships are part of everyday living in the twenty-first century.

The Bible is clear that we are made for relationship. But there is a thirst in us that no human relationship will ever be able to quench. So Jesus said.

I spent most of my childhood trying to do things in order to be liked. A shy child, I tried to counter my own insecurities by trying to be the funniest, cleverest or fastest. When I encountered Jesus as a teenager, I learned about the God who saw through my pretence and my façade. A God who saw all my faults and yet was willing to offer me complete acceptance and forgiveness. Old habits die hard, and I still found myself trying to win acceptance from people I met, but I gradually became more relaxed, more comfortable in my own skin, more myself. Happier to try things, like public speaking, which I would have found unthinkable before, I had a newfound confidence. Though not impervious to the pain of being let down or wounded by people's words and actions, I had a friend who understood. I had discovered the thirst-quenching acceptance of the all-knowing but all-loving God.

But there is a thirst in us that no human relationship will ever be able to quench.

# Thirst for knowledge

Back at the well. The line of conversation about her failed marriages had cut close to the bone. The woman was nervous. Perhaps to divert attention, she changed the subject quickly, raising the most controversial issue she could think of. The feud between Jews and Samaritans. She might as well have walked into a bar in the Catholic quarter of Belfast and sung 'Rule Britannia'. The debate was a live and emotive issue, with strong feelings all round. It all revolved around the question of the most sacred place. Jews believed the temple in Jerusalem was the central place to worship God, because that was where sacrifices were brought in worship. The Samaritans believed that Mount Gerizim was the most appropriate place to worship God.

If the woman was trying to incite racial or religious hatred, she has hit the right button – but the wrong person. In her haste to come up with a quick distraction she has inadvertently hit the exact right button. Her question about how best to worship God is exactly what Jesus is all about. Jesus honours the woman with an answer, and that answer is startling to both Jews and Samaritans. Question: temple or mountain? Answer: neither. Jesus is predicting the end of the temple and the sacrificial system. He is revealing that it does not matter who you are or where you worship God, but *how* you worship God.

Had the Pharisees been listening in to this conversation, they would probably have thrown Jesus down the well. What he is saying undermines their religious and political power structures. But actually Jesus is saying nothing new. The Old Testament is full of stories and prophets that make it clear that worship needs to be from the heart and hint at a time when God will end the sacrificial system with the perfect sacrifice.

Even now, many people fail to grasp Jesus' meaning. Worship of God is still often restricted to shrines or services or special buildings or so-called holy places. But the whole Bible teaches that these things are far less important than worshipping God by all that we are and do.

Jesus had shown the Samaritan woman respect beyond anything she had ever known. Instead of being incensed, he answered her question carefully and authoritatively. Instead of dooming her entire racial heritage, he offered a way forward. She immediately tried to make up for her outburst by bringing up something on which Jews and Samaritans agreed and, again inadvertently, she hit the exact right button. By assuring Jesus of her faith in the Messiah, God's promised King, maybe she thought she was smoothing things over. Nothing could have prepared her for Jesus' answer.

> Jesus is a revolutionary not because of military might, but because he stands up for the rights of the oppressed, welcomes the rejected and restores the broken and damaged.

'I who speak to you am he.' The first person Jesus trusted with the secret of his identity was someone considered morally suspect, socially unacceptable, second-class by race and gender. By revealing himself as the Messiah to this Samaritan woman, he showed what sort of King he is. Jesus is a revolutionary not because of military might, but because he stands up for the rights of the oppressed, welcomes the rejected and restores the broken and damaged.

This story teaches us a lot about racial prejudice, about sex discrimination, about judging people with failed relationships and about the damage done by gossip. The whole of Judea avoided Samaria, and it seems the whole of Samaria avoided the woman with the shady past. Jesus avoided neither. True followers of Jesus should also go against the flow by being ready to draw in the outcast.

The conversation has taken some strange turns. From a simple request for a drink of water, it has tracked through the deepest needs of the woman's personal life to the deepest fissures of international relations to the religious hot potato of the day to the revelation that Jesus, the tired and thirsty Jewish traveller by a Samaritan well, is God's promised King. Actually the conversation has gone full circle. Jesus' offer of thirst-quenching satisfaction is not just for the woman but for the whole community and the whole world. And now the penny drops and so does her water jar, as she realizes that the whole town needs to hear this news.

## Lifeswap – the aftermath

The story goes on:

**//** Then, leaving her water jar, the woman went back to the town and said to the people, 'Come, see a man who told me everything I ever did. Could this be the Christ?' They came out of the town and made their way toward him...

Many of the Samaritans from that town believed in him because of the woman's testimony, 'He told me everything I ever did.' So when the Samaritans came to him, they urged him to stay with them, and he stayed two days. And because of his words many more became believers.

They said to the woman, 'We no longer believe just because of what you said; now we have heard for ourselves, and we know that this man really is the Saviour of the world.' **//** (John 4:28-42)

This woman's life was transformed the day she met Jesus. She came alone, avoiding contact with the other townsfolk – used to being ignored and treated as subhuman.

She came thirsty for water and thirsty for love. But the empty water jar she brought with her to the well was left behind. It was an essential household item, but now her whole outlook on life was suddenly changed; what had seemed important before was now disposable. And what had seemed impossible before was now possible: she was no longer avoiding the other townsfolk, but actually seeking them out. She was no longer ashamed of her past, but did not mind shouting out to everybody how Jesus knew all about her. Suddenly everyone in town was listening to her story and believing what she said.

Jesus turned a socially excluded woman into the centre of her community. He turned her from one about whom tongues used to wag gossip into one whose own tongue was wagging the gospel – the good news about Jesus. He turned a desperately seeking Samaritan into a deeply satisfied Samaritan. The woman experienced unconditional love as Jesus broke all taboos in speaking to her, as he broke down all barriers in bringing up her past, and as he brought her eternal satisfaction through offering her a relationship with him.

Many people throughout the world and throughout history have had a lifeswap through encountering this satisfaction that Jesus offers. The learned C. S. Lewis would probably have identified more naturally with Nicodemus than with the Samaritan woman, but his experience of a satisfying relationship with God is vividly revealed in the way he describes the children's relationship with the God-figure of the Lion in the Narnia stories:

'If you're thirsty, you may drink.'...
'I daren't come and drink,' said Jill.
'Then you will die of thirst,' said the Lion.

**'Oh dear!' said Jill, coming another step nearer. 'I suppose I must go and look for another stream then.'**

**'There is no other stream,' said the Lion.[2]**

It never occurred to Jill to disbelieve the Lion – no one who had seen his stern face could do that – and her mind suddenly made itself up. It was the worst thing she had ever had to do, but she went forward to the stream, knelt down, and began scooping up water in her hand. It was the coldest, most refreshing water she had ever tasted. You didn't need to drink much of it, for it quenched your thirst at once.

**Notes**

1. See Chuck Swindoll, *Strengthening your Grip*, Zondervan, 1986.

2. C. S. Lewis, *The Silver Chair*, Geoffrey Bles, 1953; Puffin Books, 1966.

# blink

I wish I could believe,
but how can I deal with the tragedy of life?

Friends of mine had a beautiful baby boy. He was the pride of his parents and the envy of their friends. Happy and contented, with such beautiful dark eyes, it was impossible for your heart not to melt and your face not to smile. When he was nine months old, he went into hospital to have a routine operation. The operation was successful, but during his recovery his oxygen supply was briefly cut off and his brain was damaged. Nobody could tell his distraught parents the extent of the damage, but his limbs were stiff, his sight and hearing seemed to have been lost, and his constant crying betrayed the pain he was in.

The next few weeks and months were devastating for his family. They had to come to terms with their bereavement and learn to love and accept the suffering little boy they were now responsible for. To their quest for the reason why this had happened to them, family members from the other side of the world offered the only explanation they knew. They said it could only be a punishment for dreadful sins they had committed in a previous life and that now they had to accept this terrible shame they had brought on the family. But karma brought the grieving parents no comfort, only condemnation.

Many of us know what it is like to visit friends in similar situations and feel that nothing we say could bring any comfort or closure. Whether it is a child with an incurable condition, a devastating diagnosis later in life, or the sudden death of a friend, our hearts want to shout out 'Why?' Perhaps we have some theories to hand from our own experiences of suffering. Perhaps we too are on a quest to find out why the world is so full of tragedy.

Many people feel that the problem of suffering is conclusive proof that God doesn't exist. But when terrible things happen, often the first question we ask is 'Why?' When the medical professional tells us something along the lines of 'because the brain has been deprived of oxygen for longer than the recommended timescale', this does little to satisfy our question. We want more than a physical explanation. Our question 'Why?' exposes our belief that suffering, illness and tragedy shouldn't happen. This is not the way things ought to be. When we ask 'Why?' we are usually asking 'Why has this been allowed to happen?' Suffering and death feel strangely unnatural and unfair. The instinctive response is inner outrage; that the world is not meant to be like this. This feeling does not make sense if there isn't a God. As Richard Dawkins put it:

> If the universe were just electrons and selfish genes, meaningless tragedies... are exactly what we should expect... In a universe of blind physical forces and genetic replication, some people are going to get hurt, other people are going to get lucky, and you won't find any rhyme or reason in it, nor any justice. The universe we observe has precisely the properties we should expect if there is, at bottom, no design, no purpose, no evil and no good, nothing but blind pitiless indifference.[1]

But that doesn't feel right. It is not how most of us feel when confronted with tragedy. The question 'Why?' betrays a belief not in blind physical forces, but in an all-seeing spiritual being.

The problem of suffering and the existence and character of God go back to the beginnings of the world, and John, in his biography of Jesus, does not skirt around the issue. Jesus' next encounter brings the debate right to the fore, in a very personal way.

**//** As he went along, he saw a man blind from birth. His disciples asked him, 'Rabbi, who sinned, this man or his parents, that he was born blind?'
'Neither this man nor his parents sinned,' said Jesus, 'but this happened so that the work of God might be displayed in his life. As long as it is day, we must do the work of him who sent me. Night is coming, when no one can work. While I am in the world, I am the light of the world.'
Having said this, he spat on the ground, made some mud with the saliva, and put it on the man's eyes. 'Go,' he told him, 'wash in the Pool of Siloam' (this word means Sent). So the man went and washed, and came home seeing.
His neighbours and those who had formerly seen him begging asked, 'Isn't this the same man who used to sit and beg?' Some claimed that he was. Others said, 'No, he only looks like him.'
But he himself insisted, 'I am the man.'
'How then were your eyes opened?' they demanded.
He replied, 'The man they call Jesus made some mud and put it on my eyes. He told me to go to Siloam and wash. So I went and washed, and then I could see.'
'Where is this man?' they asked him.
'I don't know,' he said.
They brought to the Pharisees the man who had been blind. Now the day on which Jesus had made the mud and opened the man's eyes was a Sabbath. Therefore the Pharisees also asked him how he had received his sight. 'He put mud on my eyes,' the man replied, 'and I washed, and now I see.'
Some of the Pharisees said, 'This man is not from God, for he does not keep the Sabbath.'
But others asked, 'How can a sinner do such miraculous signs?' So they were divided.

Finally they turned again to the blind man, 'What have you to say about him? It was your eyes he opened.'

The man replied, 'He is a prophet.'

The Jews still did not believe that he had been blind and had received his sight until they sent for the man's parents. 'Is this your son?' they asked. 'Is this the one you say was born blind? How is it that now he can see?'

'We know he is our son,' the parents answered, 'and we know he was born blind. But how he can see now, or who opened his eyes, we don't know. Ask him. He is of age; he will speak for himself.' His parents said this because they were afraid of the Jews, for already the Jews had decided that anyone who acknowledged that Jesus was the Christ would be put out of the synagogue. That was why his parents said, 'He is of age; ask him.'

A second time they summoned the man who had been blind. 'Give glory to God,' they said. 'We know this man is a sinner.'

He replied, 'Whether he is a sinner or not, I don't know. One thing I do know. I was blind but now I see!'

Then they asked him, 'What did he do to you? How did he open your eyes?'

He answered, 'I have told you already and you did not listen. Why do you want to hear it again? Do you want to become his disciples, too?'

Then they hurled insults at him and said, 'You are this fellow's disciple! We are disciples of Moses! We know that God spoke to Moses, but as for this fellow, we don't even know where he comes from.'

The man answered, 'Now that is remarkable! You don't know where he comes from, yet he opened my eyes. We know that God does not listen to sinners. He listens to the godly man who does his will. Nobody has ever heard of opening the eyes of a man born blind. If this man were not from God, he could do nothing.'

To this they replied, 'You were steeped in sin at birth; how dare you lecture us!' And they threw him out. **//** (John 9:1-34)

 ## Blind man's bluff

Imagine living in the dark. Gail Porter, the beautiful British celebrity, took part in a televised social experiment to investigate for herself. She took on a three-day journey from Edinburgh to London wearing a pair of specially designed spectacles that simulated total blindness. Here was a simple lifeswap. Gail gave away her sight to experience life as one of the 378,000 UK residents who are registered as blind. Eventually she reached London, having undergone the frustrations of trying to use public transport blind. As she removed her glasses, blinking from the shock of the light, she broke down in tears, realizing she could do what no other blind person could do – bring back her sight in a second.

This documentary attempted to open people's eyes to the challenges of life without sight. It honoured the amazing work of those who aim to improve conditions for the blind. From the welfare state system, guide dogs charities, Braille transcribers and public awareness initiatives, there have been enormous steps forward in the last few centuries. In the first century blindness had no public champions. Life was extremely difficult. Not only were there little medical help and few educational resources, the public attitude was abominable. Blind people were believed to be cursed by God, incapable of earning and excluded from normal life. Most were forced to beg in the streets and experience the mockery of the passers-by as a daily part of life.

When Jesus and his followers came across a blind man in such a state, they saw the suffering and the followers asked Jesus the big 'Why?' question. Like most of us, they instinctively wanted to find blame for tragedy. We blame ourselves. We blame God. We blame our parents. We blame the system. We psychoanalyse. We seek revenge. We sue. Jesus' disciples had narrowed their options down to two: either his parents were to blame for his visual impairment, or he himself was.

Jesus begins his answer by refuting both options. The blame game is not a helpful place to start. Jesus explains that the brokenness of our world and the suffering we experience is not a direct repayment for a negative balance in the karma bank. As we saw in our second chapter, it was through no fault or sin of his own that Jesus suffered the persecution, isolation and desolation of the cross; he willingly put himself in our place. Jesus' unjust death on the cross demonstrates that a person's suffering is not necessarily linked to punishment for specific sins.

blink

69

So now the disciples are stumped. Their comfortable assumption that the man somehow deserved his disability had been shattered. To answer the question why this man had suffered a lifetime of blindness, Jesus gave a very strange response. He promised to use this tragedy as a means of showing God's glory and Jesus' own role as the light of the world. At first hearing this sounds as if he is turning a blind man's tragedy into a prop for a divine magic show. But what Jesus really wants to do is answer the bigger question: why there is suffering in this world. There is a connection between suffering, sin and God, but it is not as direct a link as many assume.

The Bible is clear that God made a perfect world and that it was damaged when human beings ignored God. The first sin caused a chain reaction of negative

We blame
ourselves.
We blame God.
We blame our
parents.
We blame the
system.
We psychoanalyse.
We seek revenge.
We sue.

consequences that affect all of us. We are beginning to understand some of the links; as we make connections between European deodorant use and skin cancer in Australia, for example. Who would have thought that what I do to my armpits would cause chlorofluorocarbon propellants to have a degrading impact on the ozone layer, thereby increasing ultraviolet radiation levels and cancer statistics? Our lives are intertwined. Our actions have unimaginable consequences. Most of the time we can't trace the causes of suffering. It is like looking at the aftermath of a lightning strike in a telephone junction box. All the connections are messed up, and we couldn't possibly work out where all the wires come from or lead to. Sin in the world leads to suffering, but most of the time we can't trace it back to anything specific.

Occasionally there is a direct link. If we disobey the warning signs at a level crossing and take our chances by driving onto the train tracks, there is a high possibility of immediate negative consequences as the locomotive ploughs into our car. We can't blame the train operator, who did everything he could to protect us by putting up the warning signs. The train operator gets no pleasure from watching the train being derailed and our car smashed to smithereens. Similarly, when God has warned us clearly about what we should not do in this world, and we choose to ignore those warnings, we should not be surprised at the dire consequences that follow. Many people believe God enjoys punishing us – nothing could be further from the truth. He takes no delight in watching us ignoring his warning signs, or wrecking our lives.

But most of the time the consequences of sin are much more complex. In these cases it is unhelpful to pick out certain groups or individuals and claim that their suffering is their own fault. The Bible makes reference to two tragedies in the first century that Jesus was asked to comment on. Jesus denied that the collapse of a tower, killing 18 people, was punishment on those people for things they had done wrong. And when the Roman governor Pilate murdered a group of worshippers so that their blood mixed with their ceremonial sacrifices, again Jesus said this was not because they were worse sinners than others (Luke 13:1–5). When Jesus is asked about the man born blind, he states categorically that it is neither the man's own fault, nor the fault of his family.

When Jesus is asked the big 'Why suffering?' question, he makes sure we know that the answer is not to go looking for blame, but to look for glory. Jesus turns to the man born blind and converts the tragedy of the awful impact of humanity's rebellion against God into an opportunity to show God's compassion. Jesus is going to demonstrate in a very real way what John alluded to in the first chapter of his biography: that he is the light of the world.

What Jesus does with the mud and saliva is no secret concoction of remedial elements. This is not a new kind of mud, herbal or hydro therapy. There are plenty of instances where a word from Jesus suffices to perform a miracle. Perhaps Jesus uses the mud to provide a tangible way for the blind man to know who had healed him. Perhaps he is doing this to provoke a reaction from the Pharisees. The result is the same. With a bit of spit and grit, Jesus touches the man's eyes, and when he washes it away, he can see.

Now, I must admit, I am a bit of cynic. If I had been on the street that day I would have been wondering if there was a lookalike hidden around the corner. Or if the man was a plant and had been pretending to be blind for some time, waiting for his accomplice Jesus to do the real hustle and dupe the whole town. I have a lot of sympathy with the members of the crowd that day who thought that there was some trickery or delusion going on. Blind men don't suddenly walk around having got their sight back.

Other people I know would only have needed to hear the story from a friend of a friend and they would have been calling their family to say, 'You'll never believe what I just heard...' Some of us seem predisposed to believe in the miraculous. Others are more inclined to think that miracles are impossible. Both sides are open to abuse. People who believe anything and everything can be easily manipulated into joining the latest sect or trend. People who dismiss anything and everything could be throwing the baby out with the bathwater.

A friend of mine tells the story of a class of young children invited to draw a picture of the police force. Little Johnny drew a picture of a policeman with a sneer on his face and leering eyes. Above the picture were scrawled the words 'Police is evil pigs.' The teacher was horrified and went on a public relations drive for her local law enforcement agency. A fun day at the police station was quickly organized. There were ice cream, face painting, visits to the holding cells, rides in police cars and lots of stickers. The children were then asked to draw another picture. This time Johnny drew a picture with a smiling policeman holding out a balloon and an ice cream to a happy little boy. But the teacher's face fell when she saw what little Johnny had written above the picture: 'Police is crafty pigs.'[2]

Johnny's young brain had been trained to be sceptical of the police. There was little the teacher could do to change his perception. Most of us have been trained to be sceptical when confronted with a miracle story; our minds are usually already made up. No amount of evidence is likely to change our preconceptions. And this is clearly illustrated by the crowd who watched Jesus heal the blind man. They saw the miracle happen and they fall into two camps. Some believed they had seen a miracle. Others thought there must have been a lookalike.

Some people think that those of us who live in the twenty-first century and have the benefit of hundreds of years of technological advancement can't possibly believe in miracles unlike those ignorant people in the ancient world who believed anything. This is chronological snobbery. The crowd, as John's account clearly states, was as equally divided then as it is now between those who accepted the miracle, and those who were sceptical.

John realizes that to preclude the existence of God and the occurrence of the miraculous from our understanding of the universe is simply short-sighted. He knows that many people will respond to a so-called miracle with something along the lines of 'I have made up my mind; there is no need to confuse me with the evidence.' John cleverly counters this response with clear descriptions of the unreasonable speculation of the crowds, the hyper-myopia of the religious elite and the cowardice of the blind man's own parents.

Imagine that someone you knew and respected claimed to be God and, to demonstrate the validity of that statement, to be able miraculously to make your coffee go cold in an hour. This demonstration would actually provide no evidence for supernatural ability, because the laws of thermal dynamics, convection, conduction and radiation mean that the so-called miracle is not a miracle at all. If they were to claim they could make a coffee turn instantly purple, or hum a tune, or disappear into thin air, then they would be on stronger ground as far as a miracle was concerned. However, because of a predisposition in our minds not to accept the miraculous, it would probably be dismissed as trickery.

Certainly the random coffee illustration would serve very little purpose either way. However, Jesus' recorded miracles are not random acts of power. In the previous chapter of John's biography, Jesus calls himself the bread from heaven and then proceeds to turn a child's lunchbox into a picnic for five thousand people. In the next chapter Jesus will explain he is the life-giver and then raise a friend from the dead. In this chapter, Jesus claims to be the light of the world and, the next thing we know, he is healing a congenitally blind man. Jesus uses miracles as the evidence of his identity, transcending the normal laws of nature and doing exactly what we would be looking for if the Creator of the universe were to walk this earth.

**Most of this story is actually about opening the eyes of various people in the crowd to their own prejudices.**

Jesus' miracles serve two functions. First of all, they demonstrate that Jesus is more than just a man. No first-century man with a woodwork apprenticeship would have known enough about the natural sciences to cure this man's sight. And this was no one-off coincidence – wherever Jesus went he performed miraculous healings, showing his credentials in a sceptical society. Secondly, the miracles show that in a world of crossed wires and dire consequences, God is not there to point the finger or for fingers to be pointed at. God's heart aches with compassion. When he sees suffering, he wants to interrupt the chain reaction and bring healing.

In a world where miracles are profoundly doubted, John shifts the focus onto the response to the person who performs the miracles. Specifically, this miracle demonstrates Jesus' ability to offer a lifeswap from darkness to light and challenges us to consider this lifeswap for ourselves. The darkness was not confined to physical blindness. Most of this story is actually about opening the eyes of various people in the crowd to their own prejudices.

 **The blind leading the blind**

If we were watching Jesus that day, we might have been among those who attributed this miracle to sleight of hand, or we might have put it down to supernatural power. But there are others in this story who come along after the event. The Pharisees, the spiritual leaders of the day, steeped in their own preconceptions and traditions and agendas, have to try to make sense of what they find. In many respects they are like us: cynical – rational – intrigued by a good whodunit mystery – scared of the consequences if a miracle really happened.

Of course, the Pharisees could not pull out a CCTV recording and watch the miracle for themselves. Neither could they repeat the experiment using a hundred other men born blind and a spit-and-rinse technique. The empirical method was as useless to them as it would be to me if I tried to re-create the battle of Waterloo to prove that Napoleon was defeated. In fact, if science stated that blind men do not suddenly regain their sight, all the miracle would have achieved would be to refute that law in the same way as the sudden appearance of one black swan would refute the statement 'all swans are white'. Science does not claim miracles are impossible; miracles claim scientific laws are not irrefutable.

All the Pharisees could do was to use the same technique of verification used by a law court to test the testimony of a witness in a trial. This is exactly how they proceed. The Pharisees are getting a bit of a reputation as the spiritual thought police. Nicodemus conducted his investigation at night. Now a whole group of them, with their own agendas, comes along to make inquiries. But, just as in a good TV mystery, the focus is as much on those investigating as on those who are being investigated. And the searchlight of truth actually shows up the inconsistencies and prejudices of the investigation.

The religious police bring in their first piece of evidence: a blind beggar who can see. They try to determine that he actually is the beggar who had been blind. Next, they want all the details of how Jesus performed the miracle. The man is questioned specifically about the methods Jesus used to heal him. As he describes the way Jesus used saliva and dust, stirring it up in his hands to a mixture and then painting it onto the man's useless eyeballs, the Pharisees suddenly see red. Jesus has violated a law. He worked on the Sabbath. Jesus could have healed with a command, but he stirred up trouble by mixing the mud and saliva, forcing the Pharisees to rethink the basic preconceptions of the validity of their religious system.

True, God set out the guideline not to work on the Sabbbath in the Old Testament, when he gave the Jewish nation the Ten Commandments. Those Ten Commandments and the other Old Testament laws that went with them were to enable the nation of Israel to live peaceably together and to respect God as their King. Over the years, the theologians had many discussions about the Commandments. Instead of gratefully accepting God's guideline to set aside a day off in a week, they had got into nitty-gritty debates about what actually constituted work. The Commandments turned into a thousand or more rules, and mixing mud and saliva to heal a blind man was considered an infringement. The Pharisees were in uproar that Jesus had deliberately undermined their authority by publicly breaking one of the sacred laws.

Talk about not seeing the wood for the trees! A man who has lived with the pain of isolation and the challenges of life in the dark is miraculously, amazingly, given back his sight, and all that the Pharisees can see is a possible violation of a law code they have made up. This is religion at its worst. Religion that can see only the minor infringements of ritual law instead of the bigger picture of people's lives is short-sighted indeed. Many of us have found ourselves on the wrong end of the religious professionals who seem to find only things to criticize. In fact, for some people their religion consists only of finding fault in others, an observation used by Matt Groening in his *Simpsons* cartoon. In a throw-away line, caricature Christian Ned Flanders happens to mention that his wife is away on a course to learn how to be more judgmental. However, Jesus sees through the judgmentalism of the Pharisees and challenges it by deliberately breaking the law.

Second piece of evidence: the parents. In a bid to discredit the testimony of the blind beggar, the religious police desperately turn to his parents to offer some insight. This clever bit of court drama pays off. The blind man's parents are fearful of being thrown out of the synagogue. This would not have meant simply an eviction from a building but exclusion from a community. In a highly relational and religious culture exclusion from the synagogue community would have been a catastrophic loss. So Mum and Dad play it safe and say as little as possible.

The man formerly known as a blind beggar is having a tough time. Even his parents aren't willing to stick by him and his story. His neighbours are suddenly unsure if they have ever even met him before. The religious authorities are grilling him and now, in frustration, they launch into a second verbal assault. In a blind rage, they demand that the eyewitnesses corroborate their story.

The Pharisees declare their position: that they know Jesus to be a sinner. He hasn't joined their religious group; he breaks their religious rules; he doesn't fit in their religious box; and so they condemn him, labelling him a sinner. The blind man wants nothing to do with labels. He has had his own label all his life. He just goes back to the fact of the matter: the fact that no one can deny; the fact that he was blind and now he sees.

In the eighteenth century John Newton was involved in the slave trade. He worked on the ships involved in the triangle of trafficking – taking guns, sugar and slaves between England, Africa and North America. Yet God reached out to Newton and turned his life upside down. John Newton turned from kidnapper to campaigner and from slave trader to songwriter. John Newton penned arguably the best-loved of all British hymns:

**Amazing Grace! How sweet the sound**
**That saved a wretch like me,**
**I once was lost, but now I'm found,**
**Was blind, but now I see.**

Becoming a Christian is about having our eyes opened. Not just to the truth about who Jesus is, but to the truth about who we are: how we have lived blinded by our own prejudices and blinded to the thoughtless ways we have treated God, his people and his creation.

But the words that inspired Newton, and so many Christians through the centuries, had no effect on the Pharisees. 'I was blind but now I see,' says the beggar. But the Pharisees' tunnel vision means they are only interested in the infringement of their interpretation of the Jewish law. But the blind man has seen through their questions and turns the tables on the conversation. First he subtly accuses them of being not blind, but deaf. Then he suggests that they might like to become Jesus' followers. If he is trying to provoke a response, he succeeds. They are not about to let go of their beliefs. They refuse to see Jesus' credentials. They are locked into their old ways of thinking, blinded by tradition, blinkered by their own prejudices. They throw the now sighted man out of the synagogue, condemning him to isolation and rejection once again.

Religion often uses its power and reputation to oppress, subjugate and judge, with the effect of excluding people from the church community rather than welcoming them in. But this is not the Christianity that Jesus models. He tried to free the blind man from rejection, not cause him more persecution. The bravery the man showed as he faced the angry religious authorities not with violence but with clear, cool-headed logic, with convincing argument and with courage was to act as a model to many.

**Becoming a Christian is about having our eyes opened.**

This encounter shows us how Jesus' offer of a lifeswap is double-edged. Jesus' offer of new life gives incredible healing of some of life's biggest problems, an ultimate satisfaction and a fresh start, as we saw in previous chapters. However, it can also mean abandonment by family, lack of recognition by neighbours and interrogation and exile from the community.

## Lifeswap – the aftermath

'There can be as much value in the blink of an eye as in months of rational analysis.'[3]

Malcolm Gladwell's eye-opening book *Blink* explores many of the prejudices we have adopted intuitively and many of the subconscious conclusions we come to. It challenges us to face up to some of our unhelpful implicit associations using a simple test.[4] I was shocked by my own test results. Even though I am strongly opposed to racism, was a victim of racist bullying as a child and proactively promote equality at all levels, my results showed me that I made an implicit connection between bad and black and between women and domestic life. I would recommend that others take the test, as the results are surprising: prejudice blinds us all.

Gladwell also uses many stories to illustrate the fact that over-analysis – even by experts – can overlook what is obvious to the onlooker, even untrained, after only a few seconds. His opening story tells of art experts who fail to spot a fake after a good deal of exposure, and compares their conclusions with those of ordinary passers-by, many of whom identified the replica with a simple glance.

This story of the blind beggar challenges our prejudices. Do we, like Jesus, offer the same respect to everyone regardless of whether they have shoes on their feet, money in their pockets, or referees on their CVs? Do we have time to spend talking to and helping beggars on the street, or do we walk by? Do we, like the Pharisees, have the time of day to consider Jesus, his miracles and their implications, or do we simply dismiss them as unlikely stories from an untrustworthy source?

This story of the blind beggar challenges not only our prejudices, but also our conclusions. Have we made up our minds about Jesus without sufficient attention to the evidence? Have we dismissed miracles as impossible? Have we dismissed Jesus' teaching and example because they take us too far out of our comfort zone?

Jesus challenged the status quo of his day. It was not politically correct to talk to or touch the beggars at the side of the street. It was certainly not theologically correct to heal on the Sabbath or to challenge the Pharisees' nonsensical teaching of what constituted worship and what didn't. Anyone who follows Jesus needs to emulate his compassionate approach to the rejected and his challenging

> Do we, like Jesus, offer the same respect to everyone regardless of whether they have shoes on their feet, money in their pockets, or referees on their CVs?

approach to the religious. As Jesus follows up on his encounter with the beggar, we learn more about what it means to be a Christian – in both the worship we offer and the way in which we treat people.

> **// Jesus heard that they had thrown him out, and when he found him, he said, 'Do you believe in the Son of Man?'**
>
> **'Who is he, sir?' the man asked. 'Tell me so that I may believe in him.'**
>
> **Jesus said, 'You have now seen him; in fact, he is the one speaking with you.'**
>
> **Then the man said, 'Lord, I believe,' and he worshipped him.**
>
> **Jesus said, 'For judgment I have come into this world, so that the blind will see and those who see will become blind.'**
>
> **Some Pharisees who were with him heard him say this and asked, 'What? Are we blind too?'**
>
> **Jesus said, 'If you were blind, you would not be guilty of sin; but now that you claim you can see, your guilt remains.' //** (John 9:35–41)

This is the most unusual of all the accounts of miracles in the New Testament. Normally the healing is the end of the story, but here it has been the beginning. The blind man has had his eyes opened to the truth about Jesus and he has seen the blindness of others who refused to see. He has seen the cost of following Christ. Now Jesus re-enters the scene.

Jesus heard that the Pharisees had excluded the healed man and seeks him out to ask a revealing question: 'Do you believe in the Son of Man?' This is the rescuer predicted in the Old Testament: the one who would open the eyes of the blind, heal the lame, sort out injustice, bring back the lost and fulfil all the hopes of the Jewish nation.

Like the rest of the Jewish nation, the blind man is desperately longing for the identity of the Messiah to be revealed. When Jesus claims to be that Messiah, the man takes Jesus at his word. He has seen enough. He knows that he will have to face the consequences, but he immediately and publicly worships him. The Pharisees, who are inevitably loitering to try to catch Jesus out, have also seen enough. In horror they shut their eyes and minds to Jesus' claims.

Jesus' words ring true: the blind see, and the sighted become blind. Jesus, the light of the world, shines in a dark place. John's first chapter started with a prediction that some would run to the light. Others would retreat into the darkness. Some would recognize him. Others would refuse to receive him. In this story this prediction is beginning to come true.

There is another story, about a young woman driving home late one dark night. She pulls in to a petrol station, fills up her tank, pays and gets back in the car. A few hundred yards down the road she notices in her rear-view mirror that another car has pulled out of the garage and is accelerating quickly behind her. The car sits on her bumper – lights blinking and horn blaring. She drives faster and faster, trying to escape her pursuer. She finally ends up in a ditch and cowers behind the steering wheel as her pursuer pulls up behind her and jumps out of the car. She can see in the wing mirror the man running towards her. The young woman screams as he pulls open the door and drags her out of the car. Then she sees, from the corner of her eye, the man with a knife in the back seat of her car. Her pursuer had been trying to rescue her from the clutches of the man who had climbed into her car at the petrol station.

Sometimes we can confuse the pursuing lights in our rear-view mirror as an attacker when actually it is our rescuer. God's light pursues us, to rescue us from the real danger on our own back seat of life. We can choose to run or to surrender. The healing of a blind man on a back street in Jerusalem was fairly low-key – blink and you'll miss it. But the significance of the revelation of Jesus as the light of the world and the Messiah from God demands a closer look.

Notes

1.    Richard Dawkins, *River Out of Eden – A Darwinian View of Life*, Weidenfeld & Nicholson, p. 155.

2.    Story told by Richard Cunningham.

3.    Malcolm Gladwell, *Blink – The Power of Thinking without Thinking,* Penguin, 2006, p. 17.

4.    www.implicit.harvard.edu

# pulse

## I hope there is more to life than death!

**W**hen the munitions factory blew up the fall-out was devastating. Five people were killed that day, including the person responsible for the discovery of TNT – an explosive concoction more powerful than dynamite. The headline on that fateful day in 1864 read: 'The Merchant of Death is dead.' Normally people fear to speak ill of the dead, but whoever wrote the obituary felt no restraint. It went on to say: 'Dr Alfred Nobel, who became rich by finding ways to kill more people faster than ever before, died yesterday.'[1]

The trouble was that it was not Alfred Nobel who lay on the slab in the mortuary, but his younger brother Emil. So when Alfred got up the next morning, alive and well, he found himself reading his own obituary. And Alfred was shocked to read the damning evaluation of his life and its dire verdict. All his pride in his scientific achievements dissolved instantly, as he saw that his contribution to society was exclusively destructive. That day part of Alfred died. Determined that his own close experience of death would change the rest of his life, Dr Nobel set up a fund to recognize outstanding contributions in the four fields of physical science, chemistry, medicine and literature. But the fifth and most prestigious prize was to be awarded to the person who had made the greatest contribution in the furtherance of peace. Nobel took 31 million krona accrued from his development of arms and tried to offset his shameful past by investing it in the lives of those who sought to bring peace. Alfred Nobel stared death in the face and reconsidered his life and legacy. Death gave Alfred Nobel a lifeswap.

## Dead already

Death is not a pleasant subject, but taking a good look before our obituary is written may actually change our life. In this chapter we will see what happens when Jesus stares death in the face, the face of one of his closest friends.

Now a man named Lazarus was sick. He was from Bethany, the village of Mary and her sister Martha. This Mary, whose brother Lazarus now lay sick, was the same one who poured perfume on the Lord and wiped his feet with her hair. So the sisters sent word to Jesus, 'Lord, the one you love is sick.'

When he heard this, Jesus said, 'This sickness will not end in death. No, it is for God's glory so that God's Son may be glorified through it.' Jesus loved Martha and her sister and Lazarus. Yet when he heard that Lazarus was sick, he stayed where he was two more days.

Then he said to his disciples, 'Let us go back to Judea.'

'But Rabbi,' they said, 'a short while ago the Jews tried to stone you, and yet you are going back there?'

Jesus answered, 'Are there not twelve hours of daylight? A man who walks by day will not stumble, for he sees by this world's light. It is when he walks by night that he stumbles, for he has no light.'

After he had said this, he went on to tell them, 'Our friend Lazarus has fallen asleep; but I am going there to wake him up.'

His disciples replied, 'Lord, if he sleeps, he will get better.' Jesus had been speaking of his death, but his disciples thought he meant natural sleep.

So then he told them plainly, 'Lazarus is dead, and for your sake I am glad I was not there, so that you may believe. But let us go to him.'

Then Thomas (called Didymus) said to the rest of the disciples, 'Let us also go, that we may die with him.'

On his arrival, Jesus found that Lazarus had already been in the tomb for four days. Bethany was less than two miles from Jerusalem, and many Jews had come to Martha and Mary to comfort them in the loss of their brother. When Martha heard that Jesus was coming, she went out to meet him, but Mary stayed at home.

'Lord,' Martha said to Jesus, 'if you had been here, my brother would not have died. But I know that even now God will give you whatever you ask.'

Jesus said to her, 'Your brother will rise again.'

Martha answered, 'I know he will rise again in the resurrection at the last day.'

Jesus said to her, 'I am the resurrection and the life. He who believes in me will live, even though he dies; and whoever lives and believes in me will never die. Do you believe this?'

'Yes, Lord,' she told him, 'I believe that you are the Christ, the Son of God, who was to come into the world.'

And after she had said this, she went back and called her sister Mary aside. 'The Teacher is here,' she said, 'and is asking for you.' When Mary heard this, she got up quickly and went to him. Now Jesus had not yet entered the village, but was still at the place where Martha had met him. When the Jews who had been with Mary in the house, comforting her, noticed how quickly she got up and went out, they followed her, supposing she was going to the tomb to mourn there.

When Mary reached the place where Jesus was and saw him, she fell at his feet and said, 'Lord, if you had been here, my brother would not have died.'

When Jesus saw her weeping, and the Jews who had come along with her also weeping, he was deeply moved in spirit and troubled. 'Where have you laid him?' he asked.

'Come and see, Lord,' they replied.

Jesus wept.

Then the Jews said, 'See how he loved him!'

But some of them said, 'Could not he who opened the eyes of the blind man have kept this man from dying?'

Jesus, once more deeply moved, came to the tomb. It was a cave with a stone laid across the entrance. 'Take away the stone,' he said.

'But, Lord,' said Martha, the sister of the dead man, 'by this time there is a bad odour, for he has been there four days.'

Then Jesus said, 'Did I not tell you that if you believed, you would see the glory of God?'

So they took away the stone. Then Jesus looked up and said, 'Father, I thank you that you have heard me. I knew that you always hear me, but I said this for the benefit of the people standing here, that they may believe that you sent me.'

When he had said this, Jesus called in a loud voice, 'Lazarus, come out!' The dead man came out, his hands and feet wrapped with strips of linen, and a cloth around his face.

Jesus said to them, 'Take off the grave clothes and let him go.' //

(John 11:1-43)

Mary. Martha. Lazarus. Siblings. Three of Jesus' many friends. They were especially close to Jesus and so, when Lazarus fell ill, the sisters sent a message to Jesus to let him know. At the very least, they expected Jesus to drop everything to join them at the bedside. At best, they hoped, Jesus would heal him, just as they had seen him heal countless others. But despite receiving the message in good time, Jesus waited around a couple of days, and then slowly ambled back to Bethany, where they lived. Meanwhile, the sisters were watching their brother grow weaker and weaker, powerless to help, waiting in vain for Jesus to turn up. By the time Jesus eventually arrived on the scene, he had missed Lazarus' illness, his demise and his funeral – by four whole days. Imagine the anguish. Imagine the disappointment, knowing they had been let down by the friend they had trusted to come to their rescue.

I sat at the bedside of that beautiful boy whose brain had been damaged after the routine operation and, holding his mother's hand, I prayed that he would regain his sight and mobility. I sat by my own bed after watching the television reports of the Tiananmen Square massacre, and the hostage crisis in School Number 2 in Beslan, and prayed that God would stop the bloodshed and save the children. I have prayed far less noble requests: for light traffic when I am late for a meeting; for help in my work; even for fine weather. And sometimes when I pray, it seems as though God is not going to come through for me.

When our prayers go unanswered, it can feel as if God doesn't care, and the pain of this is sometimes overwhelming. The Bible acknowledges this pain. Many of the songs recorded in the book of Psalms are written by people calling out to God, wondering where he is and why he does not answer their cries of help. These psalms reflect our own impression of stony silence from heaven. In this story of Lazarus and his family, we get a unique behind-the-scenes look at what God is doing, and why our prayers are sometimes left hanging.

Jesus is with his disciples when he receives the message of Lazarus' sickness, and yet he waits. It is not because he is afraid or unable to go back into Judea because of the death threats from that region – nothing can stop him going there in the end. It is not because he does not understand the severity of the situation – in fact he knows that Lazarus' condition is terminal.

Sometimes, when we pray, we wonder whether God is unable to act, or if he doesn't understand the situation. But the Bible is clear that God is all-powerful and all-knowing. Unanswered prayer cannot be due to some shortfall in God. Neither is unanswered prayer due to some shortfall in our prayers. Some people imagine prayer to be like an automatic cosmic vending machine, where we programme in our requests, stick in our coin of faith and then pull the lever, and out pops what we ask for. Others imagine prayer to be like a magic spell, where we say the right words in the right way and abracadabra: our answer appears. Neither of these pictures is remotely accurate.

Unanswered prayer is not due to God's inability to act or care, nor to our own inability to say the right words in the right order. The key to the problem is to understand prayer as an integral part of our ongoing relationship with God. This relationship with God is an important theme in John's Gospel. It is introduced in the first chapter, when John described how to be adopted into God's family. It is reiterated in the encounter with Nicodemus, when Jesus shows the inadequacy of religious ritual and the need for a life-transforming relationship. At the well, the Samaritan woman's thirst for relationships could only truly be met when she began relating to Jesus. At the temple, the blind man chose a relationship with Jesus despite paying the price of the loss of relationship with others around him. The overarching theme of all these

Everybody else may think Jesus is tardy and rude, offering too little too late, but Jesus has his finger on the pulse and is actually one step ahead.

encounters is Jesus' message that God loves the whole world and invites each of us into relationship with him.

Once we understand that a crucial aspect of the Christian life is this vibrant life-changing personal relationship with God, then, as in all relationships, the need for communication is vital. Prayer is this means of communication; it includes recognizing mistakes and asking for forgiveness, expressing love, gratitude, excitement, or despair and requesting help and support.

In this story we see Mary and Martha sending a message – in effect their prayer – to Jesus, informing him of their need and waiting for him to turn up. Trusting people when they don't do what we ask or expect is the real test of any relationship. When God doesn't answer my prayers in the way that I want, I have a choice: to write him off as a bad friend, or to trust that he really does care and that he knows best how to handle the situation.

Often the story ends there, as we watch, and wait and trust, as the situation either improves or worsens. In this story, we watch the situation going very quickly downhill, seemingly past the point of no return, when suddenly Jesus arrives and works a more amazing miracle than anybody ever imagined.

Jesus' own behind-the-scenes explanation of why he is waiting to go to be with his friends at this critical time is very intriguing. His disciples have no idea what Jesus is talking about when he tells them that he is waiting for Lazarus to fall asleep. First they take his euphemism for death as literal sleep, which they say will be good for him! Secondly, they realize that they are all in mortal danger if they head back to Judea, where there had been recent attempts on Jesus' life. Thomas, who has the word 'doubting' added to his name by his present-day obituary, lives up to his reputation and mutters something about following Jesus and going to die with him in dangerous Judea. But whether this is pure pessimism or uncharacteristic prophetic heroism, Thomas still sees death as the end, even with Jesus around.

But Jesus is clear. Lazarus is dead, and Jesus is not afraid of death – either Lazarus' or his own. In fact, Jesus waited deliberately, is glad he waited, and is going to Bethany in his own time to show God's glory. So, two days after receiving the urgent message calling for his attention, the son of God responds and heads towards his friends' house. Everybody else may think Jesus is tardy and rude, offering too little too late, but Jesus has his finger on the pulse and is actually one step ahead.

Funerals in the West tend to be very restrained and quite sanitized. We wait to get over the initial shock and organize the funeral for a short period of mourning at a time that suits the family. We use language that is easier for us to deal with, such as 'passed away', 'lost' or 'departed'. The deceased person is dressed and made up to look lifelike, or is hidden in a closed coffin. Graveside services are becoming rarer, and cremation is made easier to handle by a large curtain that hides the fact that the body is being burned in a furnace. Emotions are held back, and private rooms are offered to those who are not managing to suppress the tears.

Funerals in the Middle East are very different. They happen almost immediately after death, because of historical lack of facilities to prevent decomposition before burial. They last a long time, and people are not afraid to show their emotions. In fact, at Lazarus' funeral it is highly likely that most of the village would have turned up in black, joined in the loud wailing and shrieking and stayed there for the four days of misery.

Mary and Martha are grieved not only by the death of their brother, but also by apparent betrayal by their close friend. Sometimes when our friends let us down, our immediate reaction is to cut them out of our lives, determined to have no more to do with them. This is how Mary reacts initially. She has lost her faith and respect in Jesus, and because he abandoned her, she now abandons him. How tempting it is to give up when we pray for peace, but get suffering, or when we pray for a marriage partner and get singleness. Martha, however, does not treat Jesus like that. She retains enough respect for him to go and meet him when she hears he is in town, to address him respectfully, to tell him truthfully of her pain and disappointment, to confidently state her trust in him as a healer and to give Jesus the chance to give the other side of the story.

Sometimes when our friends let us down, our immediate reaction is to cut them out of our lives, determined to have no more to do with them.

Two sisters. Both bereaved and grieving. One can face Jesus. One can't. The Bible is very realistic about what people are really like. There is no dressing up to make each character a hero – they are all pathetically normal, doubting, struggling and arguing. It is wonderfully reassuring to read about the sort of people we can actually relate to. But even more reassuring is the gentle and compassionate way that Jesus deals with both his friends.

With Martha, he answers her question and rewards her faith with the promise of the hope of resurrection. With Mary, he initiates reconciliation and shows his own vulnerable empathetic grief at the death of her brother.

During the course of these conversations, both sisters find themselves in the tension common to many believers. We know that God has the power to answer our prayers, but we don't know why he doesn't. We feel the desperate hope, and we feel the pain and disappointment. We feel our faith waver between trust and doubt. The hope Jesus offers Martha has often helped Christians to hold on to their faith despite all sorts of tragic circumstances they have found themselves in.

Jesus introduces this hope when he states: 'Your brother will rise again.' This was probably the first-century equivalent for 'I'm sorry for your loss,' or 'I'm sure he's in a better place.' A platitude invented for funeral etiquette by many Jews who believed that the dead would rise at the end of time to face God's judgment. But on Jesus' lips it takes on a new significance. Martha affirms that she believes promises like the one found in the Old Testament (in Daniel 12:13) of a final resurrection, but Jesus knows that some vague agreement with theology is not a life-changing hope.

A man walked into York district hospital, put on a white coat and a stethoscope and went visiting patients. He sat by the bed of a family whose son was terminally ill and told them the great news that their son was going to recover. The parents were relieved and elated. They cried for joy. But a few days later the boy was dead, the doctor had vanished and they cried again, this time in bitter disappointment. The doctor had been an imposter. He had simply walked in off the street, impersonated a medic and offered a fragile family a false hope. The comfort he offered was worse than no comfort at all.

Jesus did not want to offer Martha a false hope, or even a vague one. He offered her a definite promise of life after death: a lifeline in her grief. He wanted Martha to know that the hope of resurrection was not some dim hope for the faraway future, but was standing right in front of her.

What did this mean? Jesus was making the incredible claim that he is the one who will bring the dead to life. He is the one who makes resurrection at the end of time possible. He is the one who will judge all people at the resurrection. He is the only one who offers that hope for life beyond the grave. Martha says yes, she understands that Jesus is the Messiah, the Christ, the one God had promised to send, the one who can really do all these things, including raise the dead.

**There had been a four-day wait and a four-day wake, but in just three words, Jesus reverses the effects of death, decomposition and disease.**

The afterlife is not a popular subject. For some of us it is easier if we believe death is the end. It is very hard for some to believe in things we cannot see or test. It is very hard to think that there may be some accountability for the things we feel we have got away with, or have thought and said in secret. It is very hard to see beyond the pleasures of this life.

On the other hand, many of us hope that there is life beyond death. We like to imagine our loved ones watching us from somewhere and that perhaps we can be reunited one day. We like to hope that our life could count for something in the grand scheme of things. But whether we hope that death is the end or not proves nothing. Our preference about immortality does not alter reality. When Jesus talks about life beyond death, he also provides compelling evidence that his claims are true.

The first thing Jesus does is break down in tears. 'Jesus wept' is the shortest verse in the Bible and one of the most puzzling. Jesus confidently waits too long to return to Bethany and determinedly goes to raise Lazarus from the dead. He says he is glad about all of that when he is talking to his disciples. But when he sees Mary's grief and disappointment, the agony of the friends and their desperate distress at the graveside, Jesus wept. His weeping conveyed at once his human vulnerability to pain and grief, his divine compassion for his friends and his heartache that this was not the way the world was supposed to be.

Imagine Leonardo da Vinci seeing his precious Mona Lisa slashed with a knife and torn to shreds. This pain at the pointless destruction of a masterpiece could well be how Jesus felt, looking at the world he created. As he saw the impact of death on his friends, on Lazarus' family and on the community, it was a stark reminder to Jesus that death was not natural or normal. It was not the way life was supposed to be. Death was the result of humankind's rebellion against God, as the only punishment for treason. So Jesus, like Mary, felt an overwhelming sense of disappointment and betrayal that brought him to tears.

I wonder if this challenges our view of God? Jesus demonstrates that God is not distant and uncaring, watching people die as though it were as mundane as switching off a light. We have seen Jesus, weary and thirsty, asking a Samaritan woman for a drink. Now we see Jesus emotionally vulnerable, in tears at a funeral, broken-hearted. God became human and was subject to the whole spectrum of human emotions. God understands the grief of bereavement and does not put a brave face on things or maintain a stiff upper lip, but publicly cries over tragedy.

Now Jesus provides evidence of his claim to power over death. He walks over to Lazarus' tomb and asks for the stone to be removed from the entrance. Even Martha's faith cannot stretch beyond the stench she imagines after four days of decomposing flesh in a hot climate. Jesus prays, showing that God the Father was working with him, and then he calls Lazarus and tells him to come and see his own funeral.

Some Jewish traditions maintained that it took the soul three days to leave the body, so Jesus' decision to wait four days may have been a deliberate plan, so there could be no doubt that Lazarus was as dead as he could be. There had been a four-day wait and a four-day wake, but in just three words, Jesus reverses the effects of death, decomposition and disease.

It is hard to imagine the scene in Bethany at the moment the dead man comes out of the grave. What the friends and family witnessed was not a hallucination or resuscitation, but a resurrection. Not through artificial respiration, or electroshock treatment, but simply through the words of Jesus. Everything obeys Jesus' words – even the dead.

Death is humankind's biggest enemy. All our power, technological, financial, or social, has no sway over death. We are powerless when we come face to face with the cold harsh reality of mortality. Yet all that Jesus does is speak Lazarus' name, and he can begin his life again, having experienced four days of death. Lazarus emerges from the tomb and from his bandages healthy and well, with his blood pulsing through his veins and his heart beating. Martha's and Mary's hearts must also have been beating very fast, as they saw their prayer finally answered in the most amazing and dramatic way. Their trust in Jesus was not misplaced. I wonder how long the celebration in the village went on for?

## Lifeswap – the aftermath

I was in the hospital for twelve long hours. While my little boy was in theatre, I walked around the ward. Babies in incubators. Babies in the arms of their parents and grandparents. Babies in body casts. Babies in distress. I talked to the families, some of whom had been there for weeks on end, some of whom expressed faith in God, others of whom expressed faith in the doctors. I prayed hard as the predicted 90-minute surgery turned into two hours; then two and a half; then three. Finally, the doctors arrived with the good news that all was well. Several hours later, and he was discharged. But as I reversed out of the car park, exhausted and relieved, I heard the crunch of the car as the post that had been hiding in my blind spot decided to crash into us. My mind raced through my bank balance, my insurance company, my spouse's reaction. On any other day I would have been distraught. But on a day when I had watched tiny lives hanging in the balance, dented metal was no big deal.

Following Jesus should enable us to keep this perspective at all times. Death and tragedy are all around us, but we have nothing to fear. Materialism is all around us, but we have nothing else to gain when there is life beyond the grave.

**//** Six days before the Passover, Jesus arrived at Bethany, where Lazarus lived, whom Jesus had raised from the dead. Here a dinner was given in Jesus' honour. Martha served, while Lazarus was among those reclining at the table with him. Then Mary took about a pint of pure nard, an expensive perfume; she poured it on Jesus' feet and wiped his feet with her hair. And the house was filled with the fragrance of the perfume.

But one of his disciples, Judas Iscariot, who was later to betray him, objected, 'Why wasn't this perfume sold and the money given to the poor? It was worth a year's wages.' He did not say this because he cared about the poor but because he was a thief; as keeper of the money bag, he used to help himself to what was put into it.

'Leave her alone,' Jesus replied. ' It was intended that she should save this perfume for the day of my burial. You will always have the poor among you, but you will not always have me.'

Meanwhile a large crowd of Jews found out that Jesus was there and came, not only because of him but also to see Lazarus, whom he had raised from the dead. So the chief priests made plans to kill Lazarus as well, for on account of him many of the Jews were going over to Jesus and putting their faith in him.// (John 12:1-11)

Lazarus dies and lives to tell the tale. Some months later, Jesus revisits the family and, not surprisingly, the sisters put on a meal in Jesus' honour. Mary has definitely understood that death is not the end. She no longer has any use for the burial perfume that she had been saving for Jesus' funeral – and in a symbolic declaration of her hope of the resurrection and an extravagant act of grateful worship she pours the precious perfume over his feet.

The Pharisees were so angry and jealous of Jesus and the publicity that the resurrection of Lazarus had caused that now even Lazarus had been added to their death list. Lazarus' rescue from human death was only temporary, and we are not told when or how he finally died. His resurrection was not the resurrection that Jesus is offering to all of us. That is a permanent resurrection, with a brand new body and to a new place after death. But Lazarus is an example, a scale model, and evidence that Jesus has the power to rule over death and offer real hope in the face of death.

Jesus' encounter with Lazarus showed a lifeswap all about hope. Hope for Lazarus and hope for Mary and Martha. Hope for the dead and hope for the living. Jesus helps us to confront our own mortality, but also our own immortality. If we can trust Jesus' character and trust Jesus' promise, then knowing that there is life after death will profoundly affect our life before death. By believing in Jesus now we can start a kind of life that death cannot take away from us. We begin a life like Jesus', that is not hampered by the fear of death. We begin a life like Jesus', that can initiate reconciliation. We begin a life like Jesus', unafraid to be open with our emotions. We begin a life like Jesus', of showing people the real hope of this life.

**Notes**

1.    Frederic Golden, 'The Worst and the Brightest', *Time Magazine*, 16 October 2000 (see also http://www.time.com/time/magazine/article/0,9171,998209,00.html).

# choice

To be honest,
my life is OK;
I don't really need God...

**H**is heart was racing as he stepped off the transatlantic flight. He had been dreaming about this moment for months. Stepping out into the sunshine, he felt a million miles away from his former dreary life. Goodbye, miserable England. Hello, happy Los Angeles! He just felt bad for his kids. But it wasn't his fault he had fallen out of love. He hadn't expected to find true love on the internet. But the stunning blonde had taken a real interest in him. She had been happy to chat to him for hours on end, and they had just clicked. When he had looked around at his own life and compared it with the pictures she had sent of her idyllic life in an amazing apartment overlooking a sunkissed beach, he knew the dream could be his. So he had left a note on the mantelpiece, packed his suitcase and caught the plane to a new life. As he looked around the arrivals lounge for the face he knew so well, for the face he had fallen in love with, she was nowhere to be seen. But there was a woman holding a sign with his name on it. The face didn't match the photos. Neither did her figure. His mind raced. The woman with the sign was looking at the ground, too embarrassed to catch his eye. The family back home had been traded in not for a dream, but for a lie.

Some of us are like the man walking off the plane. We know the pain of making wrong choices. Stuck in a job that did not live up to expectations. Stuck in a loveless marriage. Stuck with the consequences of being in the wrong place at the wrong time. Some of us can relate more to the abandoned wife and family, whose life was turned upside down through no choice of their own. Some of us know what it is like to be left for someone else. Some of us have experienced the humiliation of being edged out of our homes, jobs, friendship groups or families.

John's descriptions of lifeswaps have so far been positive examples of the changes an encounter with Jesus offers. In the next story, however, the lifeswap offer is not quite so well appreciated.

**//** Then the Jews led Jesus from Caiaphas to the palace of the Roman governor. By now it was early morning, and to avoid ceremonial uncleanness the Jews did not enter the palace; they wanted to be able to eat the Passover. So Pilate came out to them and asked, 'What charges are you bringing against this man?'
'If he were not a criminal,' they replied, 'we would not have handed him over to you.'
Pilate said, 'Take him yourselves and judge him by your own law.'
'But we have no right to execute anyone,' the Jews objected. This happened so that the words Jesus had spoken indicating the kind of death he was going to die would be fulfilled.
Pilate then went back inside the palace, summoned Jesus and asked him, 'Are you the king of the Jews?'
'Is that your own idea,' Jesus asked, 'or did others talk to you about me?'
'Am I a Jew?' Pilate replied. 'It was your people and your chief priests who handed you over to me. What is it you have done?'
Jesus said, 'My kingdom is not of this world. If it were, my servants would fight to prevent my arrest by the Jews. But now my kingdom is from another place.'

'You are a king, then!' said Pilate.

Jesus answered, 'You are right in saying I am a king. In fact, for this reason I was born, and for this I came into the world, to testify to the truth. Everyone on the side of truth listens to me.'

'What is truth?' Pilate asked. With this he went out again to the Jews and said, 'I find no basis for a charge against him. But it is your custom for me to release to you one prisoner at the time of the Passover. Do you want me to release "the king of the Jews"?'

They shouted back, 'No, not him! Give us Barabbas!' Now Barabbas had taken part in a rebellion. // (John 18:28-40)

Throughout John's biography, Jesus has been challenging the religious norms: from turning ceremonial water into wine to being seen talking with a divorcee from Samaria to healing a blind man on the Sabbath. So it comes as no surprise to learn that the Jewish authorities finally came up with an excuse to arrest him on the charge of blasphemy. However, in order to be finally rid of the uncomfortable preacher, they had to ask permission from the Roman governor Pontius Pilate, who had authority over the occupied territory.

However, Jesus was no threat to the Roman governor. He was a peaceful healer and teacher, who simply antagonized the Jewish spiritual elite. But the Pharisees were dead set. They were not after a trial, but an execution. And not only an execution, but the most brutal of all the methods used – a crucifixion.

The Romans usually kept crucifixion for those of low status, such as non-Roman dangerous criminals and slaves. It was designed for maximum humiliation, maximum pain and maximum impact as a warning to the crowd. The criminal was stripped naked, held aloft for all to see and tortured to death through impaling nails and suffocation.

For the Jews the idea of crucifixion was particularly abhorrent, because within their law there was a stipulation that 'anyone who is hung on a tree is under God's curse' (Deuteronomy 21:22–23). Crucifixion represented a horrific punishment, physical torture and spiritual isolation.

So Pilate, sitting in the governor's palace surrounded by all the trappings of authority, calls the chained, beaten, penniless son of a carpenter Jesus of Nazareth into his presence, to examine the charges and find out directly if he is about to crucify the King of the Jews.

Jesus, who showed no deference to the authority of Nicodemus, no fear of the death threats in Judea and no concern for political correctness at the well in Samaria, holds his own before Pilate. Jesus speaks his mind and challenges Pilate to make his own mind up too; not just to go along with the crowd in order to avoid rocking the political boat.

Pilate, the one who seems to have the power, is also the one who is being manipulated by the religious authorities. Jesus, the one who seems to have no power, is the one free to speak and question and challenge. Pilate has all the authority of Rome behind him and thinks he is in control of this life-and-death decision, yet feels the need to defend himself. Jesus has all the authority of heaven behind him and all authority over life and death, but feels no need to defend himself. Jesus, barely minutes away from his death sentence, calmly turns the question of authority over the Jews back onto Pilate. Pilate is indignant, backtracks sharply and tries a different line of questioning, based around not who Jesus is, but what he has done.

We too have a choice to make.

But Jesus now goes back to the question of his identity, his claim to be King. First he declares that he does indeed have a kingdom, but that it is not from this world. Jesus' kingship was not based on earthly power politics. Jesus is the King of heaven. This is a direct challenge to Pilate's authority – and to Pilate's comfort zone. Earthly kingdoms are a question of power and the Roman Empire is supreme, but Pilate does not even believe in a divine kingdom, much less know how to conquer it. Secondly, Jesus explains the nature of his kingdom: it needs no violent means to become established. Jesus' followers are not supposed to take up arms to fight for their right to rule. Jesus is not going to establish his kingdom through coercion but through conviction, and all those seeking the truth will listen to Jesus and follow him. For Pilate these are unsettling claims. His role as the governor in trials such as these is supposed to be to uncover the truth and act accordingly. Jesus is claiming superior authority (heaven over earth), superior methods (peace over war) and superior knowledge (truth over confusion), as well as a superior following (those who recognize truth over those who recognize the sword).

Pilate probably felt that he was on trial. On trial for usurping power over a foreign territory, using the 'might is right' philosophy to conquer a weaker nation through violence and the sword. On trial for daring to make life-and-death decisions when, to be honest, he did not know the truth, but had to condemn men to execution based on the testimony of a few right-wing politicians with their own agenda.

All this talk of kings and kingdoms might sound strange to us today. In the twenty-first century commitment to monarchy is at an all-time low. The idea that privileges of sovereignty simply come down to whose ancestor married into the right family tree or won the right battle is not a very popular concept. But Jesus' right to rule is not in the end based on ancient lineage or financial or political leverage. Jesus' right to rule is based on who he is. He is the Creator, Owner and Caretaker of the universe, who understands us better than we understand ourselves. He has the power, the knowledge and the compassion to rule the world perfectly.

 ## Jesus' choice

Jesus, however, chose to give up his power to become human. He chose to be born into a poverty-stricken backwater, to endure the rejection and humiliation of the people he had created, to heal the sick and help the poor. And after all that, to end up on trial, chained up and dressed down.

Pilate and Jesus. Worlds apart. Kingdoms apart. Yet the puny, insecure man is interrogating the Son of God. One Christian theologian described this bizarre scenario as a bit like a father holding up his baby daughter and allowing her to hit him around the face. Jesus, who made the genetic code that brought Pilate into being, allowed him to sit in the conqueror's palace while he himself waited for the death sentence. In fact this illustration can be used against all of us. Jesus, who brought us into being, allows us to continue rebelling against him, and to judge for ourselves for or against him and his claim to be our King.

We too have a choice to make. Elsewhere Jesus famously claimed to be the way, the truth and the life. In other words, Jesus claimed to be the only way to heaven. When John called Jesus 'the Word' in his introduction to the biography, it was because Jesus wants to communicate with us, not through a text message, DVD or podcast, but through his real life history on this planet. Like Pilate, we are faced with two glaring questions. Who is Jesus? And what has he done? And we are faced with Jesus' answers: that he represented God on earth as he interacted with people from

Everyone is so busy going with the flow that it is possible no one has checked where the flow is going.

every walk of life – the powerful and the powerless, the social elite and the social outcast – helping, healing, showing selfless generosity and courageously challenging the accepted norms.

 ## Pilate's choice

But Pilate reacts in the same way as many do today. He chucks Jesus' answers back in his face with a philosophical question that brushes the real issues under the carpet. 'What is truth?' he asks derisively as he leaves the room, not waiting to hear the answer. For Pilate, truth was most inconvenient. He was not interested in truth; he was interested in what worked. He needed to find out what he could get away with; what would get the Jewish leaders off his back; what would earn him the most votes. With a sudden brainwave, he finds a way out of making the decision. It was customary during the festive season of Passover to release a prisoner, so Pilate decided to ask the audience for a decision. He went straight to the crowd and offered them a choice. There would be an execution and the crowd could decide between Jesus, the man he realized was innocent of crime, and Barabbas, a convicted terrorist. Pilate bowed to the crowd: too cowardly to sit down and think things out for himself, he did the politically correct thing and went with mass opinion.

Sometimes Pilate's choice feels like the easiest way to get by in life. Don't waste time thinking about uncomfortable decisions and even more uncomfortable consequences. Just toe the politically correct line. Go with the flow. Don't rock the boat.

But we need to watch out, because everyone is so busy going with the flow that it is possible no one has checked where the flow is going. Everyone is so busy trying not to rock the boat that it is possible nobody's checked whether the boat is afloat.

We need to consider seriously the questions raised by Pilate. Who is Jesus? What has he done? What is truth?

But we also need to consider the question raised by Jesus when he challenged Pilate on whether what he was saying about Jesus was his own idea. Many people dismiss Jesus because of somebody else's opinion. Many reject Jesus because of the crowd.

I remember hearing about a man who always snipped the ends off raw bacon rashers before putting them in the frying pan. When asked why he did it, he explained that it was the way he had always seen his mother prepare the bacon. When his mother was asked why she did it that way, she replied that her mother had done it that way. Finally, the grandmother was tracked down and asked why she cut the ends off the bacon. She explained that she had had only a small frying pan, and it was the only way the bacon would fit in to cook. Three generations of wasted bacon ends later, the tradition was found to be pointless!

choice

**117**

Much of what we learn, think and choose in life is passed down through unexamined assumptions, values and prejudices. And these culturally transmitted habits stop many people from properly exploring the validity of Jesus' claims.

Jesus claimed to be the truth – the answer to life's ultimate questions. Jesus claimed to be sent from God the Father to communicate with humanity in relationship with us. Jesus claimed to offer a fresh start to all who have failed to measure up to God's perfect moral standards. Jesus claimed to offer a satisfying life inside us that will last for eternity. Jesus claimed to have power over death itself.

 **The crowd's choice**

What follows in the rest of John's biography is the ultimate test of Jesus' claims. Either Jesus or Barabbas was about to be condemned to death. Pilate's offer of a Passover pardon draws our attention to the timing of the trial of Jesus. John deliberately emphasizes the festival throughout the next few chapters, and by digging a little deeper, we can discover why.

Passover was the most important of the Jewish festivals. It commemorated the historical release of the nation from slavery to Egypt a couple of thousand years before Jesus was born in Bethlehem. Moses, God's appointed leader of the nation at that time, had repeatedly requested the Pharaoh of Egypt for the release of the slaves, but each time Pharaoh had refused, God send a plague on the Egyptians. The tenth and final plague was to be the worst, as Moses prophesied that each Egyptian family would lose its first-born son. This was hard – but possibly poetic – justice after Pharaoh's ethnic cleansing of Israelite sons in paranoid panic that the Israelites would eventually outnumber the Egyptians. A way out of the judgment was also offered. If a family killed a lamb and painted its blood on the doorposts, God would consider that lamb an appropriate substitute for the life of the son. That was the first Passover, as the judgment passed over the Israelite houses with the blood on the doorposts, but took out the Egyptians' first-born sons. In the aftermath of that terrible plague, Pharoah finally gave the go-ahead to Moses to take the Israelites out of the country.

The first Passover saw the substitution of the life of a lamb for the life of a son. Thousands of Passover celebrations later, in the city of Jerusalem another substitution is being offered: the life of Barabbas, the convicted murderer, the insurgent who had acted as a terrorist against the Roman authorities; or the life of Jesus, the Son of God, the teacher, the miracle worker, the one accused of claiming to be God.

The crowd's choice: Jesus, or Barabbas? The king of the Jews, or the enemy of the state? The holy man, or the terrorist? The peacemaker, or the warmonger? Napoleon once famously said:

> Well then, I will tell you. Alexander, Caesar, Charlemagne and I myself have founded great empires; but upon what did these creations of our genius depend? Upon force. Jesus alone founded His empire upon love, and to this very day millions will die for Him.

It is true that millions have died for following Jesus; but that day in Jerusalem, the crowds wanted Jesus dead. With the ultimate insult, they chose to condemn Jesus in favour of Barabbas.

What had happened to the crowd since the previous chapter, where John records people cheering Jesus on as he entered Jerusalem? A hero's welcome reminiscent of a coronation march was offered as Jesus came into the capital not in a royal carriage or on a warhorse, but on a donkey; not with arrogant pomp and show, but in gracious humility. The ancient prophecy was fulfilled:

> Rejoice greatly, Daughter Zion!
> Shout, Daughter Jerusalem!
> See, your king comes to you,

righteous and having salvation,
lowly and riding on a donkey,
on a colt, the foal of a donkey. // //
(Zechariah 9:9)

Perhaps the crowds were expecting Jesus to go on and take Jerusalem by force, overthrowing the Roman Empire. Perhaps they were expecting Jesus to be the one asking the crowds what he should do with Pilate, chained, beaten and begging for mercy. Perhaps, in their underestimation of Jesus' strategy, they felt disillusioned and angry.

So the crowd chooses to reject Jesus and call for Barabbas to be set free. Jesus' life is to be substituted for Barabbas. Barabbas walked away that day, narrowly escaping a death sentence he deserved, at the expense of Jesus' innocent life.

 ## Our choice

That day, the crowd could have chosen to recognize Jesus as King, or to reject him as a con. It is the choice that all of us face. Either Jesus is who he claimed to be, or he isn't. If he is, then we should bow to his rule in our lives. If he isn't, then we are at liberty to dismiss him as a historical let-down, as the Jews did that day in Jerusalem.

## Lifeswap – the aftermath

John is careful to tell us what happens to people after their encounters with Jesus. Nicodemus clearly becomes one of Jesus' followers. The woman at the well clearly has her life transformed and immediately spreads the good news. The man born blind worships Jesus and is not afraid to speak out. Mary, Martha and Lazarus are moved to sacrificial worship because of what he has done in their lives. But John says nothing more about Barabbas, and we have to assume from John's silence and early church history that Barabbas did not become a follower of Jesus, despite watching him literally die in his place. Barabbas encountered the lifeswap offered by Jesus, but walked away. Pilate encountered Jesus, but turned away. The crowd encountered Jesus, but threw him away.

Barabbas, Pilate and the crowd are typical of many people who know the facts about the death of Jesus on the cross, but do not grasp its significance. Jesus deliberately and willingly went to Jerusalem, knowing that he would be killed. He had the power over death and injustice, but he let them attack him with full force. Jesus allowed himself to be crucified, not just so he could take the place of Barabbas, but so he could take the place of all of us. As his blood poured down the post of the cross, God's punishment passed over all those who would ever trust in him for their rescue. Jesus was the ultimate Passover lamb, substituted willingly, innocently, for us. The cross has a central place in Christian architecture, worship songs and theology as the place where the love of God for the world is most clearly demonstrated.

Our choice is either with the millions who have subsequently grasped the significance of Jesus' death on the cross, or with the millions who have subsequently rejected his claims to be the rightful King of the universe. The choice we make has consequences. For those who wish to take up the lifeswap Jesus offers, we begin a life following his lead, seeking to be like him: offering compassion to the needy,

> Jesus was the ultimate Passover lamb, substituted willingly, innocently, for us.

choice

**121**

unconditional love to the outcast, challenge to the abusive powers, generosity to the poor. We begin a life of freedom, satisfaction and hope.

# start

Is it too late
for a whole
new me?

123

**S**ix in the morning. The clock radio bursts into song, waking Phil with a start. Sonny and Cher's 'I got you babe' plays cheerily while Phil miserably gets ready for his least favourite day of the year: 2 February in Punxsatawney. It's not a good day for this arrogant, cynical out-of-town weather presenter. He steps in a puddle; falls out with his producer; bumps into an old acquaintance he had been hoping to avoid; is confronted with the meaninglessness of his job; and can't leave town because of the weather. His only consolation is that at least he knows that, when he puts his head on the pillow, he can forget about the horrors of today and wake up to a brand-new tomorrow.

Six in the morning. The clock radio bursts into song, waking Phil with a start. Sonny and Cher's 'I got you babe' plays cheerily while Phil gets up to face another day. It's déjà vu for breakfast, followed by same-old same-old, topped off with a rerun of his previous day's mistakes, added to which is his frustration that nobody believes him when he says he has been here before. No matter what Phil does, he is not just stuck in backwater Punxsatawney, but stuck in Groundhog Day. Phil pinches himself, shakes himself, kidnaps the groundhog, even kills himself, to no avail. Phil tries to enjoy it, trying self-indulgence, outrageous womanizing and crime, knowing that nothing he ever does will have any long-term consequences. But the repetition eventually forces him to re-examine his life, pursuing new talents, becoming more heroic, more compassionate, more loving. Only when his life has changed sufficiently for him to be able to profess true love for his producer is the cycle broken. The movie finally ends with Phil waking up on 3 February a new man. A lifeswap in a day.

It is not too hard to sympathize with Phil in this film. I get up at the same time every day; eat the same breakfast cereal; walk past the same shops; catch the same train; sit on the same seat; and go to the same office, where I meet the same people. Life can feel like a scratched CD playing the same song over and over. Inescapable monotony, as the days run into one another.

Unlike Phil, we do not have several years of time warp in which to perfect the art of living a single day. Part of the repetition is the fact that I also come home at the end of the day with the same regrets. I wish I had said something; or said something different. I wish I could have done something; or done something different. I wish I hadn't missed all those opportunities. I rewrite arguments in my head. (Of course, I always win then.) I replay the football match over in my head. (This time I don't miss the open goal, but score the winner.) But life is not a rehearsal. Life has no rewind button or time-warp function. Life is a one-way journey, and so we live with constant regrets, guilt and the feeling of failure.

Our last encounter in the book of John is between Jesus and a fisherman called Peter. Peter has a similar déjà vu experience to Phil from Groundhog Day, and a similar lifeswap in a day, but, unlike Phil, has a story that frees us from regret, guilt and failure.

**Life can feel like a scratched CD playing the same song over and over.**

Peter is not exactly hero material. With a character not too dissimilar from Phil the weather man, Peter the fisherman is naturally self-centred and prone to speak before he thinks. He tends to get things wrong more than he gets them right, and if he were being interviewed for a job his CV, his track record and his personality would all naturally work against him. But when Jesus was recruiting his disciples, he earmarked Peter for the job of key leader of the early church.

Some people believe that the first Christians made up the whole Jesus story to start a new religion. But Peter's story is evidence that the Bible is historically accurate. Only in real life would such an unlikely character take a lead role. Only with Jesus around would there be such a dramatic lifeswap.

Jesus first met Peter through an introduction by Peter's brother Andrew. Jesus then recruits Peter after an unsuccessful fishing trip, when Jesus turns up to advise the professional fishermen to cast their nets on the wrong side of the boat. Having laboured all night with nothing to show for it, they express their concerns but have nothing to lose. Soon the nets are too heavy for them to lift into the boat, which begins to sink with the weight of the fish.

Peter's encounter with Jesus makes him realize that Jesus is more than just a wise religious teacher and he himself is less of a fisherman than he thought. So Peter leaves his nets and starts a new career as a follower of Jesus. Peter was undoubtedly with Jesus when he travelled through Samaria and changed the life of a woman by the well. He was undoubtedly with Jesus when he changed the life of a man born blind by healing him. He was undoubtedly with Jesus on that day in Bethany when Lazarus came back from the dead. Peter saw Jesus do many other miraculous and amazing things and saw many people's lives changed.

So three years later, when Jesus, the night before his arrest, announces that one of his followers will betray him, Peter is so convinced of his allegiance to Jesus that he publicly and confidently asserts that even if all the other disciples abandon Jesus, he never will. Jesus turns to Peter and tells him that, even before the night is out and the cock crows, he will have betrayed him not once but three times.

Peter refuses to believe Jesus and, when the guards come to arrest him, Peter tries to prove his allegiance by defending Jesus with the sword, slashing off the ear of one of the high priest's security detail. Expecting a commendation for bravery, Peter gets a dressing down from Jesus, who heals the man's ear. Peter slinks off into the night, and John's biography poetically tells the story of Jesus' trial interspersed with three stories about Peter.

As Jesus is dragged before the high priest, Peter is dragging his feet in the cold night. It is just before dawn that he approaches a charcoal fire to warm himself, where a servant girl asks if she recognizes him as one of Jesus' gang. Peter categorically denies it.

As Jesus endures his interrogation alone, calmly choosing not to defend himself against the charges, Peter still lingers by the fireside, hiding in the small crowd. But when Peter is questioned by one of them gently whether he is one of Jesus' followers, Peter vigorously defends himself against the charge.

As Jesus is physically assaulted and tortured, a relation of the man whose ear Peter cut off asks if he didn't spot Peter in the garden during the arrest. Peter denies it again.

Then, perfectly on cue, the cock crows, announcing the dawn and the truth of Jesus' prediction.

While Jesus hangs on the cross, Peter is nowhere to be seen. The women who followed Jesus are there, but the one who promised he would never abandon Jesus has gone underground. Peter does not hear Jesus' climactic cry of victory 'It is finished' as he completes his mission, fulfils the ancient prophecies and opens the way for forgiveness with God. Three days later, Peter is sitting dejectedly with the other disciples, wondering what they should do now their leader is dead and buried. Suddenly one of the women bursts in with the news that grave robbers have stolen Jesus' body. Peter goes straight to the tomb, peers inside and holds the strips of linen that held Jesus' body. Then Peter heads back home with his friends, to hide out in case the Jewish security services decide they are next on the death list. Suddenly someone else enters the room – through the locked doors.

This time it is Jesus himself standing in front of them, telling them he has accomplished peace through his death on the cross. This was not a ghost or a ghoul; not a spook or a spirit; not a hallucination or a hypnotic trance. This was not an escapologist who had performed the ultimate stunt of surviving a public Roman execution. This was Jesus, who had been dead and had conquered mortality. This was Jesus, passing on the baton of his mission to his apprentices before returning to be with God in heaven.

That would have been a heroic finale to the story of Jesus' life on earth. But John records one last chapter of the story, to finish his biography in a more unusual way: with a fresh start.

> **Afterwards Jesus appeared again to his disciples, by the Sea of Tiberias. It happened this way: Simon Peter, Thomas (called Didymus), Nathanael from Cana in Galilee, the sons of Zebedee, and two other disciples were together. 'I'm going out to fish,' Simon Peter told them, and they said, 'We'll go with you.' So they went out and got into the boat, but that night they caught nothing.**
> **Early in the morning, Jesus stood on the shore, but the disciples did not realise that it was Jesus.**

He called out to them, 'Friends, haven't you any fish?'

'No,' they answered.

He said, 'Throw your net on the right side of the boat and you will find some.' When they did, they were unable to haul the net in because of the large number of fish.

Then the disciple whom Jesus loved said to Peter, 'It is the Lord!' As soon as Simon Peter heard him say, 'It is the Lord,' he wrapped his outer garment around him (for he had taken it off) and jumped into the water. The other disciples followed in the boat, towing the net full of fish, for they were not far from shore, about a hundred yards. When they landed, they saw a fire of burning coals there with fish on it, and some bread.

Jesus said to them, 'Bring some of the fish you have just caught.'

Simon Peter climbed aboard and dragged the net ashore. It was full of large fish, 153, but even with so many the net was not torn. Jesus said to them, 'Come and have breakfast.' None of the disciples dared ask him, 'Who are you?' They knew it was the Lord. Jesus came, took the bread and gave it to them, and did the same with the fish. This was now the third time Jesus appeared to his disciples after he was raised from the dead.

When they had finished eating, Jesus said to Simon Peter, 'Simon son of John, do you truly love me more than these?'

'Yes, Lord,' he said, 'you know that I love you.'

Jesus said, 'Feed my lambs.'

Again Jesus said, 'Simon son of John, do you truly love me?'

He answered, 'Yes, Lord, you know that I love you.'

Jesus said, 'Take care of my sheep.'

The third time he said to him, 'Simon son of John, do you love me?'

Peter was hurt because Jesus asked him the third time, 'Do you love me?' He said, 'Lord, you know all things; you know that I love you.'

Jesus said, 'Feed my sheep. I tell you the truth, when you were younger you dressed yourself and went where you wanted; but when you are old you will stretch out your hands, and someone else will dress you and lead you where you do not want to go.' Jesus said this to indicate the kind of death by which Peter would glorify God. Then he said to him, 'Follow me!'

(John 21:1-19)

Peter, fisherman turned disciple, now returns to fishing. Despite three years on the road with one of the most historically unique figures. Despite an encounter with the resurrected Jesus. Despite a direct challenge to carry on the mission that Jesus started. Perhaps they needed some quick cash. Perhaps they needed some down time. Perhaps they couldn't get their heads around the enormity of the task. Or perhaps there was something else nagging away at Peter's mind.

The story begins with an unsuccessful fishing trip and a stranger who turns up to advise the professional fishermen to cast their nets on the wrong side of the boat. Having laboured all night with nothing to show for it, they express their concerns but have nothing to lose. Soon the nets are too heavy for them to lift into the boat, which begins to sink with the weight of the fish. There seems to be something vaguely familiar about this scenario. Déjà vu? Suddenly Peter needs no more information. He knows exactly who the stranger is, jumps into the water and runs to shore.

Jesus is standing with a cooked breakfast ready and waiting, next to a charcoal fire in the cold. Dawn is fast approaching, and Jesus has three questions to ask Peter. Déjà vu? The last time Peter stood by a fire, the three questions challenged his allegiance to Jesus, and Peter denied having anything to do with him. Now, by another fire, Jesus asks three questions of allegiance.

'Do you love me?' These words seem strange in our ears today. But the greatest command in the Bible is to 'love the Lord your God with all your heart, soul and mind' (Matthew 22:37; and see Deuteronomy 6:5). Jesus was inviting Peter to reconsider his allegiance, and this time he calls for complete devotion. Not just intellectual assent; not just spiritual interest; not just emotional fervour. Loving God with our whole being is no spectator sport but an immersive experience of loving and following Jesus, involving all that we are.

As Peter responds affirmatively to Jesus' questions, perhaps he begins to understand their significance. The scene is set perfectly. And Peter, knowing the guilt and regret of the night of the trial, is offered the chance to relive the day of his failure in the light of the resurrection.

John had to include this chapter, because what Peter had done had been wrong, and now there was a loose thread that could be tied off, exactly because of Jesus' death and resurrection. Peter's denial had been wrong not because it broke some law or rule, but because it had broken relationships. Peter had let Jesus down. Peter had let himself down. Peter had betrayed Jesus, valuing his own safety and desires above his commitment to Jesus.

Christianity is not about ceremonies and feast days, rules and commands, philosophy and church. Ultimately, Christianity begins with a personal relationship with God through Jesus, as we have seen throughout this book. Whenever we betray that relationship by following our own needs and desires, we break relationship with God.

Jesus shows us through this encounter with Peter that this betrayal cannot be glossed over or brushed under the carpet. The damage needs to be confronted.

**Christianity is not about ceremonies and feast days, rules and commands, philosophy and church.**

I get déjà vu when I watch action movies: whether it is a 1970s Bruce Lee kung fu epic, a 1980s Chuck Norris movie, a 90s Jean Claude Van Damme blockbuster, or a twenty-first-century Jason Bourne rollercoaster ride. Their plotlines all move in a very similar direction, encountering numerous bad guys, a variety of weapons, exciting chase scenes and predictable scripting. Undoubtedly the film will start with a betrayal, and the rest of the movie revolves around the inevitable, unstoppable revenge. We cheer at the end when justice is done and the enemies have been killed. There is a certain satisfaction when the rivals confront the damage they have done and come to a terrible end.

But Jesus, confronting Peter with his betrayal, is not about to exact some awful revenge. He gently offers Peter a fresh start. There is also a satisfaction here that forgiveness is offered, but it is not at the expense of the satisfaction of justice being done, because of what Jesus has just done. We know deep down that betrayal deserves punishment; but God is able to offer reconciliation instead, because he has poured out his righteous anger on Jesus in our place, as he hung on the cross and died. Because of Jesus' death and resurrection, reconciliation is now available to all – even to unfaithful cowards like Peter.

Jesus does not deny Peter's past failures but deals with them by confronting them, taking in the slack and forgiving Peter. Instead of punishment he offers Peter the privilege of a position of responsibility.

Jesus' mandate to Peter to 'feed my sheep' is a reference to shepherding or pastoring the people who follow Jesus. In other words, Jesus was giving Peter the responsibility of leading the early church. This was a unique task, but there is a principle here that we can apply to ourselves.

When Jesus calls us from the middle of whatever we are doing, whether fishing or any other profession, pastime or activity, we can apply the same principle. Jesus will want to deal with our past unfaithfulness, offer us forgiveness and give us a privileged role to play in his mission.

If Peter had been offered the job without dealing with his past, he might have been tempted to take up the responsibility in order to make amends for his mistakes and earn Jesus' trust again. But Jesus first offers Peter a chance to declare his love and allegiance, and when Peter replies, Jesus shows him how he can demonstrate that love through service to the church.

The church is not a building or an institution, but the people of God, who are likened to sheep in need of shepherding. When we accept Jesus' offer of forgiveness, we not only reinstate our relationship with Jesus, but we join the people of God, where we can use our gifts and skills to serve one another and the world around.

However, Jesus is also clear that this service may be painful. To Peter, Jesus says specifically that he will face suffering and death. Peter, who wimped out with the first whiff of persecution when Jesus was being arrested and tried, is now being told that he will face the same public humiliation and execution. The terrible cost that is part and parcel of Peter's lifeswap freely offered by Jesus should come to us as no surprise. With the exception of Barabbas, who walked away from Jesus' offer, all the other lifeswaps we have considered have been received freely and have cost them dearly.

Jesus paid the cost, willingly relinquishing his divine rights in order to become human. Jesus gave up his perfect life to willingly accept God's punishment in our place. Jesus paid the ultimate price of his own death in order to buy us life now and life when we die.

Nicodemus came at night with his questions, but after meeting Jesus realized that as a public figure he could not keep his lifeswap a secret. At the time of Jesus' execution, most of Jesus' followers went dark, but Nicodemus, publicly and at great risk, came forward to help bury Jesus.

The Samaritan woman went to the well alone, avoiding taunting comments and looks from the other women. But after meeting Jesus, she runs into town to talk to everyone she can find. She risks the cost of what little self-respect she has left in order to take the initiative in letting all the other townsfolk know about the lifeswap Jesus has given her. She does not keep the good news to herself, but shares it willingly with neighbours she knows to be judgmental and dismissive.

Mary is distraught at her brother's death, but after meeting Jesus she is grateful beyond measure. Her life savings – in the form of expensive funeral perfume – were poured over Jesus' feet in an act of costly devotion. Nothing was too much to give to Jesus, who had given her the certainty of knowing life beyond death: the certainty of heaven.

The blind man was belittled and ostracized, but on meeting Jesus he is given the gift of sight, which should have enabled him to gain access into the temple and status in the community. These benefits are stripped from him, because he is unafraid to speak the truth of Jesus' role in his lifeswap.

What is it that makes people accept the lifeswap Jesus offers, even though it is so costly? Many Christians will acknowledge the difficulties of speaking out for their faith in public; the cost in telling their neighbours about what Jesus has done; the sacrifices they have made from their personal belongings, or their public standing; in some cases their rejection, persecution and even death. Jesus does not promise us that our new life will be easy, but he does promise that it will be whole, real, satisfying, healing, hope-filled, purposeful and eternal. This is the sort of life many of us are dying to discover.

The finale of John's biography offers a fresh start not only to Peter, but to anyone who is willing to encounter Jesus, acknowledging their faults and recognizing that Jesus has the power to forgive and transform.

## Lifeswap – the aftermath

Peter failed miserably. He was a flawed fisherman and a defective disciple who betrayed his master and friend. I expect Peter mulled over the events of that night between the Last Supper and the rooster's dawn chorus many times. In his imagination, perhaps, he answered those three questions differently. But just when he thought it was too late for him, Jesus came back, re-created the scene and asked Peter three new questions. Jesus was ready to give Peter a second chance; and this time Peter answered honestly.

After that, the Bible records many times when Peter was given the option to stand up for Jesus or deny him. Peter, having been given a second chance, and knowing the consequences of speaking up for Jesus, was a transformed man. He was willing to face beatings, imprisonment and eventually death in order to let the world know that

Jesus does not promise us that our new life will be easy, but he does promise that it will be whole, real, satisfying, healing, hope-filled, purposeful and eternal.

Jesus was really God, who died for the failures of us all. Peter the failed fisherman of Galilee became the founding father of the global church.

At the start of this book we saw Jesus' lifeswap, as he exchanged heaven and all its privileges for earth and all its problems. By the end of John's biography Jesus has experienced the whole spectrum of life on planet earth. We have seen Jesus hungry, thirsty and tired, bereaved and honoured, tortured and executed. We have seen Jesus cut through the niceties as he talked straight to a government dignitary. We have seen Jesus cut across social taboos as he engaged in conversation with a local outcast. We have seen Jesus deliberately flout religious laws as he heals on the Sabbath, and disappoint his friends only to prove to them the reality of the afterlife as he raises their brother from the dead. We have seen him trade places with a terrorist to free him from the death penalty, and take time out after the resurrection to seek reconciliation with a friend who betrayed him. Far from predictable, far from conventional, Jesus' lifeswap challenges our own understanding of the Jesus of history. But more than that, it challenges our own life.

Perhaps we can relate to Nicodemus: respected, educated, but never quite convinced. At the back of our minds we wonder whether there is supposed to be more to life.

Perhaps we can relate to the Samaritan woman: searching for significance through relationships, but never quite satisfied. At the back of our minds we wonder whether anyone can ever love us truly, unconditionally.

Perhaps we can relate to the blind beggar: ostracized, unpopular, the world seems to be set against us. At the back of our minds we wonder whether we will ever be accepted.

Perhaps we can relate to Lazarus – numb, dead already – or to his sisters – bereaved, and terrified at the prospect of death. At the back of our minds we wonder if there is more to life than death.

Perhaps we can relate to Barabbas: we've had a lucky break in life, and we don't feel that we need anything else. We want just to close the book and walk away.

Perhaps we can relate to Peter: constantly missing the mark, often failing. At the back of our minds we wonder why on earth anyone would even bother to offer us a second chance.

John wrote: 'These are written that you may believe that Jesus is the Christ, the Son of God, and that by believing you may have life in his name.' If we can relate to any of these people, then by seeing how Jesus transformed them we too have the possibility of a lifeswap.

John wrote:
'These are written
that you may believe
that Jesus is the
Christ, the Son of God,
and that by believing
you may have life in
his name.'

start

**139**